PRAISE FOR

MISSING SARAH

PRYOR

"A real labor of love told compellingly and honestly with emotional power."

—BELLA ENGLISH, *Boston Globe*

"Barbara's beautiful tribute to her dear daughter Sarah in this book was very moving for me. I felt like I was being allowed to enter into this family's most poignant time. I am honored to be able to read this touching story of a beautiful, witty, shy, and caring girl who was loved by so many. I cried, I laughed and I was angry at what people do.

"One of my favorite parts was when Barbara was sitting down and a butterfly hovered around only to lite on her arm and she said, 'Hi, Sarah.' It was so special. Out of the ashes comes life and this was seen as Barbara tries to be there for other people going through similar times. I especially liked all the poems and I got tearful when I read about Sarah's dog Katie and her sled created in bronze to be put in the park.

"I commend this mother for writing such a beautiful and heartfelt tribute to her loving daughter. She may have only been with us a short time, but Sarah's legacy will be here many years to come. We won't forget Sarah Pryor.

"Thank you for this intimate gift."

—GAIL REICHERT

"The book was heartbreaking at times, I felt like I could feel the pain coming through. I wanted to reach out and give the family a hug or send the mother an email letting her know the story touched me. It was inspiring to read how through her pain, she continued to reach out to others and see the good around her. As Barbara recounts her loss of her beautiful Sarah, I cannot help but be amazed by her strength. This book will make you cry, as well as make you cherish every moment with your family."

—ANGELA B

"Ahhh, I don't want to put it down. So much raw emotion. So much love. Thank you soooo much for giving me a sneak peek!"

—SARAH OHM

"I received Barbara's book on March 25th and was eager to read it. Little did I know how heart-wrenching that would be. I would read a number of pages and have to stop. I have just finished it this afternoon.

"Our family lived across the street from the Pryors in Wayland, MA. I remember vividly Barbara coming over the late afternoon of 10/9/85 to tell me that Sarah hadn't returned from a walk. I put my two small children in the car and went out looking for Sarah and went out later again that night with another neighbor. Little did we all know that event would forever change our community.

"Barbara has eloquently put into words an unspeakable event. I continually admire how she has turned her heartbreak into compassion and empathy for other victims. I am in awe that she has come to forgive the perpetrator and chosen to focus on her gratitude for all the people who have helped her in this journey. As Mr. Rogers said, 'Look for the helpers.' Barbara has indeed done that.

"God bless Sarah and her family."

—NANCY JOHANSEN

MISSING

SARAH PRYOR

Byron, niece Beth Pryor, Andy, Sarah, Meg, and Barbara visit Cambridge in 1984.

MISSING

SARAH PRYOR

A Mother's Testimony of
Choosing Love over Grief and
Emptiness

BARBARA SMITH
PRYOR

SARAH'S
SONG
PUBLISHING

The author is always happy to hear from readers. For information about special discounts for bulk purchases or author interviews, appearances, speaking engagements, or just to get in touch, please contact:

Barbara Smith Pryor
P.O. Box 4971,
Pittsburgh, PA 15206
missingsarahpryor@gmail.com

First Edition

Cataloguing: child abduction, child murder, family loss, community loss

Edited by Elizabeth Philipps and Rodney Miles
Cover design by Anka Kovacevic and Rodney Miles
Jacket design by Rodney Miles
Book and page design by Rodney Miles
All images © the author unless otherwise noted
Missing Child poster design by Jerry Cibley

In honor of Sarah Elizabeth Pryor

You taught me your lessons

of unconditional love

and abundant joy,

and for asking me,

"Mom, what if the sun comes out today

and melts the snow?"

Your forever song plays on in the hearts of many.

Dedicated with love to Sarah's brother and sister,

BYRON and MEG.

You stand tall in spite of sorrow, hurt, and anger.

You love in spite of countless questions unanswered.

You encourage me, and I love you.

"A successful life is not about dying. It is about living well. I have known two-year-olds and nine-year-olds who have changed people and even entire communities by their ability to love, and their lives were successful though short. On the other hand, I have known many who lived much longer and left nothing behind but emptiness."

—BERNIE S. SIEGEL, MD
Author, *Peace, Love, and Healing*

"Without memory, there is no healing. Without forgiveness, there is no future."

—ARCHBISHOP DESMOND TUTU

CONTENTS

PROLOGUE:

SARAH IS NOT

FORGOTTEN

MY SATURDAY MORNINGS begin early with weekend errands to tackle. This particular day I realized I had to cram six tasks before noon when my friends Carol and Cindy would stop to pick me up for our visit to a friend who had recently relocated into an assisted living facility. First on the list was a planned hair cut with my talented and cheerful 21-year-old hairstylist. There was just one person ahead of me, a 40-something gentleman. I saw his hair was fairly short and he most likely needed only a trim which would mean I could be in the chair fairly quickly. I sat listening as they chatted and I heard my hairstylist ask a question that caught my attention:

"How are you going to celebrate Thanksgiving?"

"My wife, my daughter and I," the customer said, "are going to visit relatives in Boston."

This piqued my curiosity as I had lived in the Boston area for 13 years before returning to my native Pittsburgh in 2000. I was getting ready to self-publish a non-fiction book about my nine-year-old daughter's abduction in Massachusetts in 1985. I pulled out a business card and wrote the title of the manuscript on the back of the card:

MISSING SARAH

A Mother's Testimony of Choosing Love over Grief and Emptiness

I got ready to introduce myself to the man once his haircut was finished. I would say that I was familiar with Boston and would give him the card to share with his Boston relatives who most likely would know the Sarah story.

"Thank you," he said, "and Happy Thanksgiving."

I sat in the chair to have a quick trim and was soon out the door and on my way to the grocery store. When I finished the morning errands it was afternoon and my friends were impatiently waiting for me in my apartment's parking lot. We visited for a while and I returned to my apartment. It was about 3:00 p.m. I took a quick look at my e-mails before heading in for a well-deserved nap. I glanced at an e-mail from a man named Gary at 11:15 a.m. with the subject line: "Meeting Today."

I read Gary's message in amazement:

"You gave me your card this morning with the title of your up-coming book after my hair cut. I told my wife the story and she was stunned that I met you because she knew the story of Sarah's disappearance so well. She never forgot this awful event! You see she was Sarah's bunk mate at Summer's Best Two Weeks Camp (1985). She has not forgotten Sarah all these years! Thank you for stopping to tell me about the book."

In my mind, I repeated, *She never forgot this awful event, she has never forgotten Sarah.*

I am still marveling at how my impatience with a haircut could turn into an amazing blessing.

When I became a member of Eastminster Presbyterian Church in the East End of Pittsburgh in 2004, I volunteered to work on the Women's Ministry Committee. I hosted our monthly meetings in my spacious two-bedroom apartment in nearby Bloomfield. The front door of my second-floor apartment opened up into a long hallway leading to the living and dining rooms. I had filled the space on the hallway walls and on end tables in the living room with many framed photos of our Pryor family and my Smith family. Sarah's presence was suitably arranged and prominent.

One of the women in this group I enjoyed, Anne, whose talents and wit perked my spirits, was a "thirty-something." She sat across from me on the settee, me in my favorite cozy armchair. The meeting had begun and a woman named Lynn was giving a report when Anne began to sob.

"Anne, what is wrong?" I asked.

She gasped, trying to say the words, "I have something to tell you. I should have told you when I first met you. I am sorry I haven't told you until now."

"Anne you can tell me anything, please know it is okay."

"Barbara, I was Sarah's counselor at Summer's Best Two Weeks Camp, the last summer of her life in '85. When I heard she was missing, I said, *Not Sarah, not Sarah*! She was the sweetest camper I ever had. We had to write counselor letters to parents after each camp term and mostly I made up stuff to say. But not with Sarah. I meant every word."

"Anne," I said, "I still have the letter. Thank you for telling me. That you had the honor of knowing Sarah personally is wonderful. How lucky you are! Think of the hundreds and hundreds of folks that cared about Sarah but never had the joy of knowing her. You have made me very happy my dear. *You*. Come here so I can hug you."

And as we hugged I thought again to myself, *She never forgot this awful event, she has never forgotten Sarah.*

INTRODUCTION

"The brave, who focus on all things good and beautiful, give thanks, and discover joy, are the true change agents who bring fullest light into the world."

—Anne Voskamp, *1,000 Gifts*

IN THE SPRING of 1980 I attended a three-day retreat for women called *Cursillo*. "The Cursillo movement was founded in Majora, Spain by laymen in 1944 and spread from the Roman Catholic sponsorship to other Christian denominations in North America. The three-day retreat shows Christian lay people how to become effective leaders in their communities and churches with priests and lay people giving talks to participants who take what is learned back into the world on what is termed *The Fourth Day*. In other words, the rest of their lives." (Cursillo pamphlet) After that weekend I discovered a way to carve out quiet time for daily devotions and prayer.

When I was a girl growing up on a farm, I would awake to the rooster crowing in the early mornings so I knew that was a good time for me to spend an hour in solitude. Little did I imagine that five years after that Cursillo training I would stockpile stories that would become models of faith for me to remember on the frightening days following October 9, 1985. Among those stories were stories from the days of tall sailing ships, of sailors allowing themselves to be bound to a mast with heavy rope to prevent them slipping over board in violent sea storms. I pictured myself bound to a mast by a rope, woven of the prayers of many people, which would keep me safe through fierce storms. I knew that despite the turmoil I would not drown.

In the fall of 1985 we moved our family from Peter's Township, Pennsylvania to Boston for new job opportunities. Byron (17) was going to be a junior, while Meg (15) would be a freshman at Wayland High School. Sarah (9), our shy third grader, left her three best friends in Peter's Township near Pittsburgh for fourth grade at Clay Pit Elementary School. I wondered how my children would react to our moving out of state. Byron and Meg were eager to begin a new adventure, especially because four cousins lived in a near-by community. But when Sarah heard the news, she sat deep in silence and thought, remained speechless, and then began weeping.

I wrapped my arms around her. "Sweetie," I said, "what's the matter?" Sarah didn't respond. She only nodded yes when I asked if she wanted to talk about it later.

I turned my attention to the myriad details of our move. Sarah began to get caught up in the excitement of packing and didn't talk more about her feelings. We celebrated July the 4th with friends, but amid the pleasures of the holiday I was saddened to see Sarah softly crying— her brother hugging her.

1—Ruth Black gives Sarah a spa day in Pennsylvania with breakfast in bed while Barbara and Andy are house-hunting in Boston.

Then on a hot and humid day in late August, our family of five set off from the rolling western hills of Pennsylvania to Wayland, Massachusetts, a western suburb of Boston. My husband Andy drove as I sat in the front with our children in the back heading toward Massachusetts in the packed car, anticipating the move into our new home—a Cape-style four-bedroom house on Concord Road (Route 126) seventeen miles west of downtown Boston. My Pittsburgh church friends had given me a good-bye gift, a house plant set in a miniature Conestoga wagon, complete with billowy sails and wooden wheels. Attached was the message, "You are a pioneer lady, going to an unknown land. An adventure lies before you."

That first day of our journey to Boston I gazed out the window thinking that this trip was not at all like the arduous trek of the real pioneer women who traveled in Conestoga wagons long ago. There were no permanent good-byes, no unknown dangers. I had been excited as my family was beginning a new chapter.

The children started school after Labor Day. Meg and Byron easily adjusted to their high school, adding sports to their schedules. Sarah joined the 4th and 5th grade chorus and was practicing songs from the musical *Oklahoma*. Meg was blessed with a talent for singing which was not the case for her younger sister. What Sarah lacked in pitch she more than made up for with enthusiastic monotone volume.

The first Sunday in October, 1985, Mary and Carl Olson who lived next door introduced us to the neighbors by hosting a welcoming brunch for our family. They created a large poster which identified the neighbors' houses with the names of family members. Each neighbor wore a color-coded name tag that matched their house number, helping us identify them. We enjoyed good food and conversation during the friendly welcome to Wayland.

My sister Carroll, her husband Bob, and their four children lived in nearby Concord, so we began enjoying time together. Our two families shared weekly dinners around a large table accommodating four adults, four teens, and two preteens. Conversations were lively and laughter rampant. What a gift it seemed to be living within a short drive of each other's homes.

I became familiar with the best route for the 45-minute commute to my job as Director of Admissions at Bradford Business School in Boston, while Andy launched his investment broker job search. We found a new church home at the Church of the Holy Spirit and began to worship there. On September 1, 1985, the two new Episcopal Rectors, Anne and Cassius Webb, began their ministry in Wayland.

Our lives seemed settled and peaceful.

My nine-year-old daughter Sarah was kidnapped in 1985 and 13 years later, in 1998, her murdered remains were positively identified through mitochondrial DNA testing. If you have known a loss, you share a journey with me. I have changed the way I live my life because of the way my child lived her short life, and I am working through my loss in a way that works for me. I wrote this book because I care deeply about the losses you have known or will know.

Come join me. This book is written with you in mind.

PART ONE:
MISSING SARAH

[1] MISSING

Wednesday, October 9, 1985

COMMUTER TRAFFIC wasn't so bad that late afternoon going west out of Boston. Grateful for the time to decompress from the challenges of my new job, eager to find out what progress Andy had made in his job search, I had time to marvel at the beauty of long, low sunrays lighting October foliage, and to wonder how the kids' day at school had gone, especially Sarah's, our youngest, whom I had persuaded to go this morning. I walked into the house at 6:10 p.m., glad to be home and thinking about dinner. The day was quickly turning to darkness. I greeted my husband, and asked, "Where are the kids?"

"Meg's at lacrosse practice," he said. "Byron's at football practice. Sarah ate a bowl of Jell-O at about 4:00

and said she wanted to explore the neighborhood. I asked her if she wanted to take the dog with her, but she said that Katie would slow her down. Her goal today was to walk farther than she walked yesterday." Andy was worried because more than two hours had passed since she left the house and now it was chilly nightfall.

Anxious, not knowing where Sarah was, I grabbed my car keys, ran out the door, shouting, "I will go look for her." Driving north I hoped that Sarah had tried to reach my sister Carroll's house in near-by Concord. With tears and an ache in my soul, I arrived in her driveway and leapt from the car, running into the house, frantically yelling, "Is Sarah here?"

My brother-in-law Bob met me, "No, what's wrong?" I explained that Sarah had not returned from her walk. "I'll call Carroll at work and we'll come to your house as soon as we can." he said.

On the way home, I trembled, afraid something was unspeakably wrong. Back at the house, I was barely able to speak. Nonetheless I updated Andy and I phoned the Wayland Police Department to report our nine-year-old Sarah was missing. As police officers arrived at our house, I felt I was in dream, *yet it was happening to us*. Police cars parked on our front lawn as dozens of police officers, new neighbors, and church friends crowded the first floor of our home. Andy and I left the confusion of the household and walked along the path we thought Sarah had taken, holding flashlights and calling, "Sarah! Sarah!" We imagined she might have strayed off the path, fallen, and was lying somewhere injured. I didn't want to stop searching, but I knew we needed to return to the house jammed with police officers and neighbors. Carroll and Bob were there. Meg and Byron had come back from school to the chaotic scene and been gathered under Carroll's reassuring wing. We gathered family and church friends in a circle and prayed that we would find Sarah. I felt strong warm hands holding mine on both sides of me, assuring me that I could remain hopeful.

At 11:00 p.m. that night a police officer approached Andy and me with a kindly voice to tell us, "We are temporarily calling off the ground search. Know that cruisers from every nearby community will be out looking for your daughter. At dawn, we will resume the search with helicopters, canine crews, mounted police, and FBI agents." We had renewed hope and were grateful to be told the plan.

On automatic pilot, I undressed and brushed my teeth, my mind replaying the day's beginning as an ordinary day with beautiful, early fall weather. When Meg and Byron had left the house for school, I went into Sarah's room to awaken her. She surprised me, insisting she didn't want to go to school because she was being teased by a boy in her class. (Sarah was an unusually tall nine-year-old, a little over 5 feet.) With some encouragement I got Sarah to promise me she would give school a try.

I walked her to the bus, kissed her, and wished her a good day. Back at home I made a phone call to her teacher, Miss Anne McNamara, to tell of Sarah's struggle. Anne assured me she would handle the situation discreetly without Sarah's noticing. On the drive home that evening, I had anticipated asking Sarah about her day. My last thought before I tried to sleep was, *How could this day have turned so terrible?*

Thursday, October 10, 1985

THE NEXT MORNING Byron left the house at 6:00 a.m. with an apple and Sarah's jacket. He was so sure that he was going to find his sister and she would be cold and hungry. After an hour or so of searching he returned without her. We opened the door to police officers, FBI agents, and neighbors bringing food and casseroles for the freezer. Byron's friend Billy Donahue arrived with his dad Ralph having driven all night to Wayland from Pennsylvania. Meg and Byron stayed home from school and devoted themselves to greeting people at the front door.

When the noon news aired on October 10, 1985, the greater Boston area learned that a blond nine-year-old girl named Sarah Pryor was missing from Wayland, Massachusetts. And it was in the newspaper, too:

> "Nine-year-old Sarah Pryor disappears after leaving her Concord Road home in Wayland around 4 p.m. to explore her new neighborhood. She was last seen walking along Route 126 wearing her Walkman stereo headphones."
>
> —*Boston Herald,* October 10, 1985

For Mother's Day Sarah had given me a piece of her artwork. The third graders created designs from their hand and finger prints. Sarah decorated her thumbprint as a mother hen. The tips of her fingers became chicks and flowers. She called her masterpiece "You're Thumbody Special, Mommy." Five months later, Meg showed an FBI forensic team to her little sister's bedroom to dust for Sarah's fingerprints. Eyeing Sarah's artwork, an agent asked for permission to borrow the picture to create a composite of her fingerprints. I asked myself, *How could such a precious gift become so filled with pain and sorrow?*

Meg, sobbing, caught my attention, as she reached for me: "Mommy, they are ruining her room with purple dust. Please make them stop."

I was powerless to help either of my daughters. I remembered a quote by writer Gary Schteyngart: "Can you hold your own world together while the greater world falls apart?"

That second day I felt I was churning in a sea of white capped waves tossing about in a flimsy raft. I feared that I might drown unless I could think of something to help me. The memory of a talk by Alden Hathaway, the presiding Bishop of the Episcopal Diocese of Pittsburgh, came to me. He likened faith to open hands allowing us to receive abilities and talents, along with other gifts—family, friends, good health or financial success. Because we are human we grab hold thinking them our possessions. In our haste we lose sight that we are stewards of our loved ones not owners. He told us it is painful to have fingers wrenched loose from a clenched fist—painful to give up control we never really had.

In the evening, Sarah's daddy sat in his burnt-orange Lazy-Boy chair in the family room afraid to sleep for fear that she would return while he dozed on that second night without Sarah. I convinced him to move six feet, from his chair to the couch. He insisted the doors stay open and unlocked and every light ablaze. Remembering the words of Bishop Hathaway, I prayed for courage and began telling Andy the story of the "open hand." I was reminding myself that we had no control of the situation. Sarah was a gift and we must hold our hands open, and trust. I believed that God was grieving with us because perhaps someone had taken our precious one. We cried together until we collapsed in emotional weariness. He came to bed, letting me close the doors.

We slept very little that night.

"Sarah, there is nothing to be afraid of," I had said many times telling her that she had the nightlight in the bathroom as well as her small, light-up cross which was activated each night after exposing it to a light source in the daytime. She could hold the cross in her hand until day break. We climbed the stairs at 9:00 each night for prayers and a goodnight kiss. Hoping she would feel safer, I told her I'd be reading a book in my bedroom nearby. From time to time, Sarah would appear in the night at our bedside.

"Mommy," she'd say, "I'm scared. Can I sleep with you?"

I thought she was going through a stage similar to my own fears of the dark at the same age. I welcomed her to snuggle between Andy and me and she was soon asleep, the next night ready to return to her four-post bed.

Meg came to our bedroom the night after Sarah was missing asking to stay close to us. Sensing her fears, we cuddled her close. After a week in the crowded bed, Meg announced, "Tonight I am going to be brave, and return to my room. Don't be surprised if you hear a little mouse in the night. It may be me."

I thought longingly of Sarah coming to bed with us in happier days.

AS PARENTS OF a missing child we were living in unknown territory. Television and print media were at our front door as soon as Boston learned Sarah was missing. We were conflicted, wanting to cooperate but needing respect for our fragility. My perception of the media was distorted fearing the worst of them, that they would be hounding us, invading our privacy. We believed Sarah was alive and realized we needed to work with the media to have her picture and story broadcast as quickly and widely as possible in hopes of bringing her home.

The day after she was missing I volunteered to manage the relationship with the media by updating the press daily at 3:00 p.m. on the lawn of the Wayland Police Station. Chief Galvin prepared a press release but warned reporters there would no questions after it. I thanked the assembled reporters for their support, finished reading the briefing, and was relieved to hear complete silence.

Sarah's story continued often in news of the day. I told the media we wanted to cooperate with them in an effort to find Sarah, but we would need to set boundaries of what we were free to talk about and what we could not divulge in order to protect the integrity of the investigation. They were helpful in bringing the heartache of a missing child into homes throughout New England. I continued to be grateful for the partnership that grew with many of the news professionals.

One of my favorites in television media was Charlie Austin, of Boston's station WBZ. He arrived at our door, introduced himself and said, "I am so sorry for you and your family." I knew at that moment I had a special friend in the media. Charlie reported the news with accuracy while treating us with compassion as the family of a missing child. Charlie was given the Media Award for his sensitive treatment in his crime reporting at one of Boston's annual Victims' Rights Conferences. He accepted the honor saying, "After my first contact with the crime victim, I ask myself, 'Based on what you said and did today would you be asked back into their home tomorrow?' If the answer is yes, then I've done my job well." Charlie was an example of some of the fine people in the media who saw our hearts and hurts as more than just a news story. And he would appear again later, just when I needed him.

This crime hadn't happened to someone else in some other state, city, and town—this was *our* neighborhood. This wasn't an unknown little girl's picture on a milk carton—this was *Sarah Pryor*, classmate of the fourth graders at Clay Pit Hill Elementary School. This was Byron and Meg's sister, Barbara and Andrew's daughter, niece and cousin to the Pryor, Smith and Sandel families. This was Sarah's grandparents' beloved granddaughter.

And because it happened to Sarah, it could happen to anybody, anywhere.

Saturday, October 12, 1985

THIRTEEN-HUNDRED VOLUNTEERS searched 10 square miles of swampy woods in North Wayland in hopes of finding Sarah. Kind people swarmed into Wayland that Saturday, hoping to find our little girl. Throughout the day nearly 100 police officers from nearby towns and volunteers in groups of fifty searched a 10-square mile area. Andy and I were told that the officers would lead volunteers in the areas they had previously mapped. We were not told details of the planned routes. Our family greeted and thanked the many people who lent a hand— and a heart, too—to help that day. I wondered if the police invited the public to be involved because the police needed the help, or because it provided a way for people to feel useful and to remain hopeful. The search began mid-morning as groups set out under the leadership of officers. Around noon, teams returned to the church parking lot to rest and eat boxed lunches provided by several local churches.

I chatted with many volunteers and discovered that some had traveled from miles away, answering the publicized call for help. I spent the day thinking only of how grateful I was to receive the outpouring of love from so many strangers, concentrating on the goodness of people, trying not to waste a moment's energy thinking of anything else. Andy, Meg, Byron, and I mingled with searchers in the parking lot for much of the morning, then returned to our home in the early afternoon. As dusk filled the afternoon sky, I looked out the front window and spotted an elderly man with a sturdy walking stick, accompanied by a small boy, presumably his young grandson. They were two of hundreds of caring strangers, all wanting to help in this frightening, powerless situation.

At the day's end, I spoke to the crowd of searchers, thanking all for coming to search for Sarah, reminding the searchers, as I reminded myself, "Now, we are focusing on our faith and not on our fear."

[2] FEAR, DOUBT, DISBELIEF

"Show the people with a compass that still points north. A shaft of light, sometimes only a glimmer that both defines and thwarts the darkness."

—Anne Lamott, *Bird by Bird*

Sunday, October 13, 1985

THE WAYLAND POLICE Department, the Massachusetts State Police, the FBI assigned to Sarah's case and the Boston Middlesex District Attorney and his staff all worked together without boundaries in cooperative collaboration. They were a team of compassionate and dedicated investigators who relentlessly pursued their mission to bring resolution to Sarah's case while treating our family with courtesy and kindness. Although none of the team knew our Sarah personally she never was far from their hearts. I gave each member of the team a photo of Sarah which they placed on their desks or in their wallets.

Wayland is a bedroom community for Boston commuters. The schools are academically sound, the churches plentiful, and the town fairly sleepy. Andy and I met Chief of Police Gerry Galvin and investigators Sandy O'Brien and Steve Williams at the Police Station after Sarah was taken. As I walked into the meeting room I thought how naïve I had been assuming once you married and lived in the suburbs you lived happily ever after. Gerry began the meeting by suggesting that Andy and I cooperate with the media letting them talk about Sarah and display her picture in a joint effort with their department to bring her home safely. He assured us that his department would work cooperatively with the Middlesex District Attorney's Office, the Massachusetts State Police, and the FBI.

An efficient group of thirty or so investigators and criminal justice professionals was created which I labeled, "Sarah's Team." Chief Galvin said if there was something we should know the investigators would tell us. Otherwise, they would work silently and continually on every lead. Andy and I were comfortable talking with the media, but the job that proved most difficult for both of us was waiting.

In spite of Gerry's gruff-sounding-voice, I quickly came to appreciate the compassionate heart under his badge. His colleague, Sandy O'Brien, was an industrious worker with a tough-sounding voice and professional demeanor. Slowly, I began to appreciate Sandy's contagious smile and her dry humor. "Barbara, we are family," she explained one day. The third of this trio was Steve Williams with his young face and receding hair-line and a dimpled smile, often beaming back at me. He was the detective who had told me on the evening of Sarah being missing, "I promise you I will bring Sarah home." I didn't know how or when Steve would do what seemed to be impossible. But I believed he could.

Monday, October 14, 1985

AFTER THE WEEKEND Meg and Byron wanted to return to the schedules and routines at school. Life was predictable Monday through Friday—Get up, eat breakfast, go to school, attend classes, stay after school for sports, come home for dinner, do homework, go to bed and repeat the routine again the next day. Each day Andy set up job interviews and was in and out of the house during the week. I welcomed returning to my job which demanded my attention and concentration on business matters rather than wondering about Sarah. I trusted the investigators would continue working on finding Sarah and they would notify us when there was a need. I could hardly wait to fall into bed at night and surprisingly was able to sleep without having bad dreams. Meg said that she would wake each morning hoping that Sarah being gone was a bad dream and she could dismiss her fears. Sadly, we all were living a nightmare.

The weekends were the hardest without the weekday routines that took our minds from thinking that the longer it took the investigators to find Sarah the less likely there would be a good outcome. It was difficult for me to be my usual out-going personality which often celebrated the joy in living each day. I shied away from social gatherings telling Andy how hard it was for me to be away from work or home where I felt safe displaying little emotion. I didn't want to talk to others about how I was feeling nor did I want to pretend that nothing had changed in my now upside-down world. I was comfortable being quiet at home. Andy enjoyed conversing with almost anyone so it was a sacrifice for him to agree to my wishes to have limited social contact. Meg and Byron continued meeting with friends on Friday and Saturday evenings. We had dinner with my Concord family but other than that I was glad to be a homebody.

Sundays the family usually went to church but I found it hard to be around friends there, especially watching them enjoying their children while Sarah was still missing. I hurried our family home, made brunch, and prepared to go back to the routine of work the next morning.

As the oldest girl of five siblings I had learned to be responsible, keeping busy helping my overwhelmed mother with the endless chores in managing a household of half a dozen kids all born within twelve years of each other. This became a natural survival skill for me in tending to my family. My mind and my chores kept me from having spare time to worry or wonder. Now it kept me from me thinking, *What if?*

One day I retreated to our bedroom for time alone. I was emotionally exhausted yet not physically tired as I sat on my purple, flowered, quilted bedspread in this warm and safe refuge. I needed to think of the days before the beginning of this new daily walk of uncertainty. What had brought us here? Why had we come to live in New England? Thoughts flooded my mind in the room's stillness.

The move from Pennsylvania to Boston just weeks before seemed to be in another life. Now, day after day without Sarah, without answers, I started each morning feeling unbalanced and wobbly in hope. There were occasional days when I drove home from Boston and, nearing the last turn, imagined seeing police cars and television cameras on the lawn as the town turned out to celebrate her homecoming. Then I'd see the lawn just as I had left it that morning and emptiness returned to my heart.

It was a challenge for my family, adjusting to the different ways Andy, Meg, Byron, and I dealt with the dreary suspense of not having answers to Sarah's absence. The four of us seemed to eke out getting through each day. We handled our grief, fears, and sadness in private ways, rarely talking aloud about our fears, being distracted and more comfortable talking about the daily schedule—who was going where and when they would be home. Byron's two frequent questions were, "What's for dinner?" and "What time do we eat?" I stayed open to questions about Sarah or the investigation and would answer truthfully when asked, but I did not initiate conversations with Meg and Byron about her. I hated being asked, "How are you doing?" and I did not ask it of my family. Even before Sarah went missing Andy and I had trouble communicating, hearing each other, listening without being defensive. It only worsened after she was gone. Only trivial subjects remained safe in our conversations.

Meg and I have similar personalities. We process things first through our feelings. Byron is more like his Dad and uses logic to navigate through tough times. Meg told me she did not like to see me being sad because it made her think Sarah was not coming back. I didn't want to upset her. When I headed to Boston each weekday I allowed my feelings to surface and would begin to cry to and from work, wiping away tears when I returned home. I thought of naming my car The Wailing Car.

Tuesday, October 15, 1985

KIND PEOPLE SEEMED to appear in the most unlikely places after Sarah's abduction. Leo Burdick was an FBI agent assigned to the case. I had returned to work in Boston and Leo's office was nearby. Andy met me in front of the Federal Building and once we passed through security, Leo met us. He guided us through the maze of FBI offices. At first glance his size and occupation intimidated me, and I was startled to discover I stood up taller in his presence. Yet when Leo spoke his voice was gentle, like my favorite Uncle John's.

A week after Sarah's abduction his request terrified me. "It is a matter of procedure, when a child is missing, to do a routine lie detector test of the parents just to rule out the possibility that they were involved." Leo emphasized he was certain neither of us was a suspect, but protocol required him to get the results on record.

Wanting to be tested first to get the procedure over with, I was nervous that my anxiety would give a false reading, prompting the FBI to think that I could have hurt my child. A technician explained that he would ask a series of "yes" or "no" questions. While he prepared the equipment I tried to tell myself that the lie detector process was not any different than an electrocardiogram. I prayed for peace, yet I was terrified.

The questions began as facts: "Is your name, Barbara Pryor?"

"Yes."

"Do you reside in Wayland Massachusetts?"

"Yes."

Then, suddenly: "Do you know what happened to Sarah Pryor?"

My breath caught in my throat. "No."

My mind raced with fear. Was my blood pressure rising? Would they think I was not being truthful?

Quickly another innocent question came, "Are you married to Andrew Pryor?"

"Yes."

"Did you have anything to do with Sarah's disappearance?"

"No."

I began to dread the Sarah questions. Sad weariness blanketed my soul. Suddenly, my emotions turned. I was angry, screaming in my head, *Why are you wasting your time asking me these totally unnecessary questions about my involvement in Sarah's disappearance? I want you to get out of this building and go looking for my little girl. Every day we lose, lessens our chances of finding her alive!*

But, in compliance, I said only two words—*yes* and *no*.

When the ordeal ended for both of us, I regained my composure. As we drove home we knew we had passed.

AS A CHILD, being compassionate and helping others was natural for me, but letting people give to me was challenging. I thought I could do, or must do, almost everything better by myself rather than needing or asking for assistance. After Sarah was gone, I experienced such genuine caring from the people around me. Neighbors filled our refrigerator shelves. Dirty family laundry disappeared, was washed and returned clean, folded, and distributed into appropriate bureau drawers. Garbage and recycling were carefully gathered for collection.

Neighbors and church members formed a group of volunteers to be in the house during the day to answer the phone in case a call should come regarding Sarah. I was thankful that Carroll stopped by the house most days to see how she could help. The cousins kept themselves busy with school activities although I was sure their love for Sarah and each other was never far from their hearts.

The Webbs, the newly ordained couple who had begun serving The Church of The Holy Spirit six weeks earlier, were catapulted into daily service to our grieving and despairing family. The Reverend Anne Webb was at my side, often gently yet firmly coaxing me to eat when I thought I was not hungry, to rest when I thought I was not tired. I realized that we were newcomers to Massachusetts yet so many people were extending profound kindness to us. Our friends in the Pittsburgh area could not imagine how the Pryors, as strangers to New England, could be so lovingly cared for.

It is comforting and heart-warming to recount the myriad ways so many people helped with the search for Sarah. One man, Jerry Cibley from Attleboro, Massachusetts, volunteered to create and distribute posters in an effort to get Sarah's picture and information quickly and widely distributed so that more people could be looking for her. My feelings were mixed about my Sarah becoming a poster child, with her picture below the headings HAVE YOU SEEN THIS CHILD? or MISSING CHILD. The flyers appeared on toll booths, trees, telephone poles, and bulletin boards throughout New England.

When I had the joy of meeting and becoming friends with Jerry Cibley, he told me about a visit he had at his photo services shop from some police officers investigating why he, a volunteer, had produced so many posters of Sarah in his shop. Perhaps he was even a suspect for a short time. We shared a rueful smile about how his energetic kindness bore such unexpected interpretations.

Life has unfathomable ways. When Jerry wrote to me, he said, "Children are not supposed to die before their parents. Can life ever be the same or is the tenor of life impacted forever?" Years later, on Mother's Day 2007, three weeks from high school graduation, Jerry's son Jordan was killed in a car crash while talking on the phone to Jerry's wife. My friend Jerry has ever since been a committed force in the fight for stronger laws about distracted driving.

MISSING CHILD

Name: Sarah E. Pryor
Age: 9 DOB 01/13/76

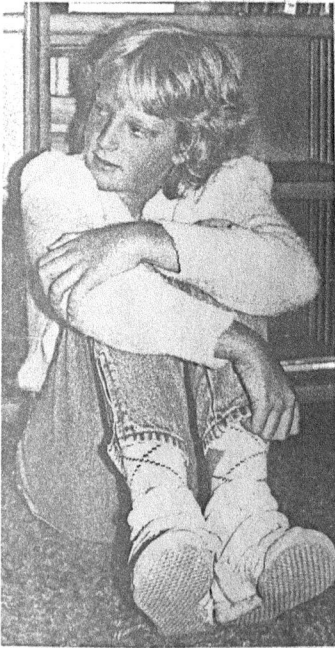

Race: White
Sex: Female
Hair: Lt Blond
Eyes: Hazel
Height: 5:2"--5'3"
Weight:100lbs
Build: Slender
Complexion: Fair

Looks age 12-13 years

Wearing blue jeans,
white sweater and
high top sneakers.

Missing from Concord
Rd. Wayland 4P.M.
10/09/85

ANY INFORMATION CALL WAYLAND POLICE

WAYLAND. MASSACHUSETTS

(617) 358-4721

2—Poster design by Jerry Cibley

[3] FAITH

Wednesday, October 16, 1985

WHEN SARAH WAS first missing I made a life-saving decision within two days. Although I felt as if my arms and legs had been torn from my body, I decided I would not be robbed of the powerful memories of my Sarah by turning my anger and sorrow inward. I would remember her loving spirit and try to show her kindness to people as they came into my life. I gave myself the gift of forgiveness, so that nothing in me would mar her sweet soul. That I have been able to do this is in large part due to the loving support and prayers of family, friends, and a host of people I have never met. Through the long years my faith has sustained me.

My sister Carroll arranged to have a neighborhood psychologist meet in our home with both families in an effort to allow Byron, Meg, and Sarah's four cousins,

Megan, Rowen, Kate, and Brendan, to share their thoughts and to ask questions. We all crowded into the living room as Dr. Carl Brotman acted as facilitator for us to share our feelings of fear, anger, frustration, sadness. The children said very little, showing their discomfort at being asked questions. The four parents were scarcely dealing with the trauma—no wonder their children could not absorb it. Dr. Brotman told the children that their parents were worried, sometimes frightened, and we all would go through many feelings. I clearly heard one statement he offered, for it reinforced that decision I had made a week before. Dr. Brotman said that persons living through tragedies tend to go in one of two directions: Either they turn their feelings inward and isolate themselves or they turn their feelings outward and focus on actions or causes that they can control or influence.

As I said, my choice was to honor my daughter's joy and kindness. I would not lose Sarah's sweet spirit and become bitter by repressing my fear, doubt and anger. I would remember her loving spirit and show that to people who came into my life. With the help of lots of people, I would turn compassion outward and work to become a beacon of hope.

SARAH'S TEACHER had one of the most difficult assignments of her teaching career. No college course could have prepared Anne McNamara for the kidnapping of one of her students. Every week after October 9th I called Anne, longing to be assured that Sarah's classmates were managing. I rejoiced to hear her say, "Things are a bit confused, but, the class is doing pretty well." Anne was gifted in communicating hard things to little ones, and at dispelling rumors. Asking her students to share what they were hearing about Sarah, she often responded with assurance: "Well, I've talked to Sarah's Mom and Dad, and they don't say that."

When I checked after Halloween, she said that Sarah's desk was the appointed place of honor for the class pumpkin. The fourth graders insisted that all Sarah's papers be stored properly in her desk awaiting her return. But the overall hopeful mood began to dissipate as Thanksgiving break approached. Anne confided that Sarah's classmates were acting out. The well-mannered were misbehaving and the more mischievous ones were becoming mean-spirited. The class had assumed Sarah was taking a short visit and would soon be back in school with them. In their innocence they could not understand why she did not return and were becoming angry. Sarah's best friend and her classmates struggled to understand what had happened to Sarah. We adults were not able to do much to help them because we were without answers.

Later when a media blitz erupted with a false report of Sarah's kidnapping, a team of mental-health professionals met at Sarah's school to prepare advice to help parents try to explain to their children the inexplicable words being used. I did not have the emotional reserve to call and talk to Anne at that time. I was trying to save my own children from the devastation of that horrible lie. Now it is a source of deep regret to me that I stopped calling Sarah's teacher.

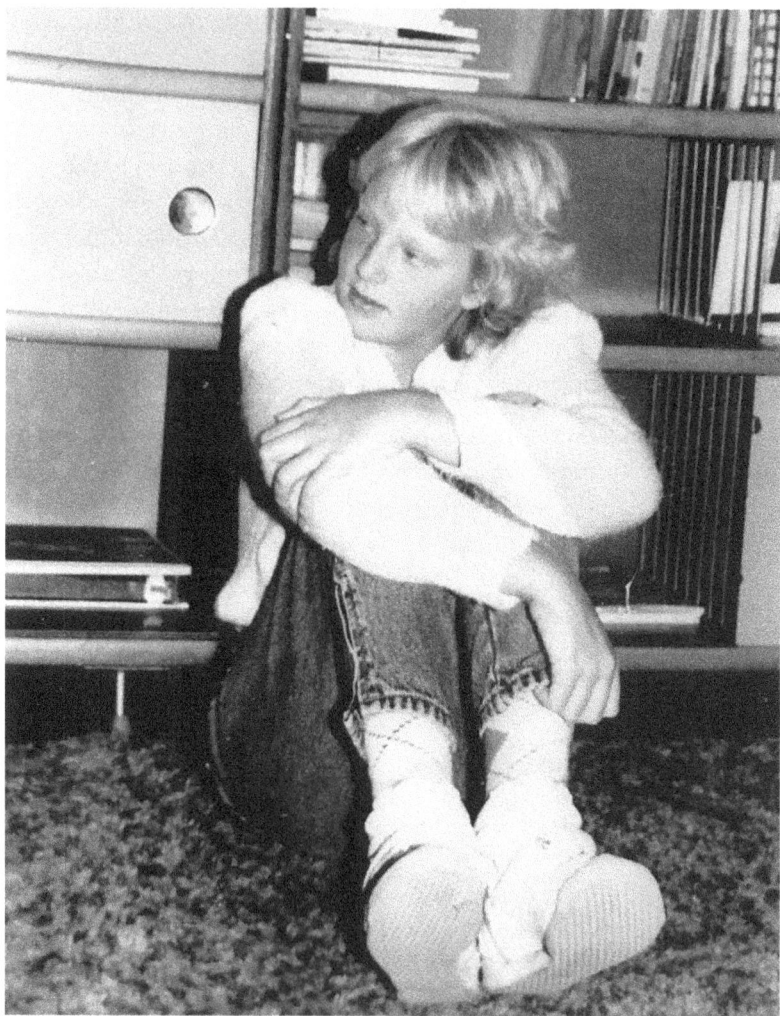

3—Miss McNamara's photo of Sarah five weeks before the abduction.

Sunday, November 17, 1985

THE HUSBAND AND WIFE ministerial team, Anne and Cassius Webb, began their Massachusetts ministry on September 1, 1985 at Wayland's Episcopal Church of the Holy Spirit. Our family started attending the church as we settled in our new home. Andy and I felt a bit awkward as newcomers when we met the Webbs for the first time—strangers meeting strangers. How soon that would change. Anne and Cassius were at the very core of our daily lives. Andy and I had been immediately struck by the couple's blending of two distinct personalities into a cohesive and complimentary unity.

Anne: straight-forward, compassionate, persistent, and quick-witted with a talent for finding humor in the ironies of life. Cassius: bright, reserved, endlessly deep, one of the few who by his quiet persistence emanates strength and invites you to partake of his peace and calm.

The first week after Sarah's abduction they were with us daily and into the evenings, answering phone calls, guarding the door from unwanted media, receiving casseroles, and making sure we ate and tried to sleep. They were there to care for us and to care about us. They were angels sent to us for our minds when we could not think and nothing made sense, our eyes when we could not see, and our feelings when we were numb.

On November 17, 1985, the Sunday before Thanksgiving, the Reverend Webbs granted Andy's request to make an announcement to the congregation. Andy said, "Our home church in Pennsylvania has invited friends to set an extra place at the Thanksgiving table and pray for Sarah. We invite you to join us as we pray for her, for all of us and all who are troubled by her being missing. We pray for the investigation and for the person or persons who took her."

Andy ended with thanks then sat down to complete silence. Cassius was not moving or speaking, and we saw tears flowing from his eyes as his usual quick mind failed him. Slowly, steadily he gave the words of the offertory and the choir began to sing. After the service ended Andy and I sought Cassius. When we couldn't find him Andy asked Anne to apologize for us.

"Better he than me," she said. "I'd still be trying to talk."

CABBAGE PATCH DOLLS were one of the most popular Christmas gifts for girls in 1984. Like so many mothers I had hunted feverishly for one. By good luck I found two dolls, one named Faith and the other whose name I have forgotten. Sarah's friend from school and her cousin Katie waited as weeks and months went by without answers to why Sarah was missing from their lives. I thought of a way to keep them hopeful and connected to Sarah by asking if each would baby sit one of her dolls, carefully adding, "at least until Sarah comes home."

Happily, the girls agreed.

We received this note from Sarah's friend from school in November:

> "Dear Mr. and Mrs. Pryor,
>
> "I just want you to know that I am taking good care of Sarah's Cabbage Patch doll. She came to church with me on Sunday for the special mass for Sarah and every night we wish that Sarah will be home soon because we miss her. She plays with my dolls while I am at school. I cannot remember her name so I call her Felipa—

is that right? Thank you for letting me babysit Felipa. I pray for you and Sarah every night."

Sarah had an endearing friendship with her cousin Katie Sandel, who was Sarah's age and temperament. As days and weeks passed without knowing what had happened to Sarah I realized how troubling it was for Katie. When I asked her to be the babysitter for Sarah's beloved Cabbage Patch Doll, Faith, until Sarah came home, she gladly agreed. Katie told her mother she was missing Sarah. Comforting her daughter, Carroll said, "We have to have faith."

Katie replied, "Oh, I go to bed every night with Faith.

"Based on an anonymous letter, the FBI and police search five Rhode Island towns, Burrillville, North Smithfield, Gloucester and Johnston."

—*Boston Herald* , December 23, 1985

"In Weirton WVA, 40 miles from her former home, police hunt for Sarah Pryor after receiving a tip from a man who said he believed he saw her eating at a Hardee's restaurant."

—December 29, 1985

"Sarah Pryor's disappearance is featured on *Missing II: Have You Seen This Person?* a nationally syndicated broadcast program on missing children."

—*Boston Herald*, January 22, 1986

[4] ANGELS

"When people love and people share, when people help and people care, when people hope, and people dare, Angels… they appear."

—K.A. Hinton

December, 1985

I HAVE KNOWN angels on my journey. None wore halos or wings, and they weren't gloriously heavenly. They were ordinary people, faithfully performing errands of mercy and love. One was a stranger named Phyllis who wrote a note from Erie, Pennsylvania, months after Sarah's abduction. Offering her sorrow at hearing of our family's loss, she continued, "I lost my husband several years ago, and I remember the *after*—after the funeral, and after my friends went back to their lives. I was stuck in the *after* and it was hard. My promise is to write just to let you know that you are loved."

Every week, without fail, a note would arrive. If I had occasional doubts that others still cared, Phyllis was my reminder.

Another angel appeared that first Christmas to help me navigate through the holiday. Louise was a spirit-filled woman, serving her family of nine children and her church with equal faithfulness. This neighbor boldly announced to my sister Carroll, "I've decided that I'm going to help Barbara by doing all of her Christmas shopping. Get her list so I can buy and wrap the presents."

This wonderful mom intuitively knew my empty, despairing heart. Having fun became foreign to my once joy-filled spirit. Louise returned several days later with packages beautifully wrapped, labeled and ready to be given. She even mailed gifts to relatives out of state. Louise gave me a priceless gift that first Christmas without Sarah. When I heard of her death ten years later, I replaced my sadness with a smile, now imagining Louise as a real angel joining the chorus with my girl.

I discovered that many male angels hovered near. Jim was one with a selfless sacrifice. He wrote that he could not imagine himself in our situation, especially because his daughter, Sarah, was also nine years old. Jim's promise was to remember us, praying daily for our family by placing a pebble in his shoe. The irritating pebble caused discomfort, as he trudged through snow, often stomping his feet, crying out in both pain and then in prayer. Jim's family told us that Jim had misplaced the pebble one day and was frantic until he located the missing stone. Years later, I learned that Jim's career in a high-tech industry took a significant detour. His caring, compassionate heart led Jim to answer a call to the ordained ministry. I smiled as I thought of Sarah Pryor's part in his new vocation.

I believe countless angels surround us at all times. Phyllis, Louise, and Jim are just three of the angels I have known personally. I am honored to have received their gifts of grace.

January, 1986

ON A PARTICULAR, emotionally-fragile day as I drove into Boston for my work, a song by Jefferson Starship, "Sara," unexpectedly caught my attention. Sadness washed over me as I heard the haunting refrain, "Sara, Sara, Sara." Relieved that I was alone and wouldn't upset Meg and Byron, I wept until I reached my parking space at work.

An hour later, my secretary announced, "Charles Austin is on the line."

Quietly, I answered, "Hi Charlie, how are you?"

"I was sitting here thinking about you," he said, "wondering how you all are doing."

"I can't believe your timing, Charlie, I'm not doing very well. I cried all the way to work again. I'm not afraid of letting the sadness come."

"What are you afraid of?" he asked.

"I'm afraid of being afraid!"

"Barbara, close the door to your office. Sit and let your fear overwhelm you for a moment. Don't fight it. Let it come and then let go of it!"

With Charlie's advice, I gave myself permission to acknowledge that I was scared. I confronted my sadness, then I looked directly into the eye of fear, saying to myself, *You can do this!*

IN JANUARY, a particular edition of the *Family Circus* comic addressed child abduction and I just had to write to the cartoonist, Bill Keane:

"Dear Mr. Keane,

"As a mother of a child missing since October 9, 1985, your Family Circus cartoon, appearing in the Sunday, Boston Globe January 19, 1986 touched my heart. Some people feel we are frightening our children unnecessarily and it would be best not to talk about the possibility of people taking them. I wish I had talked with our Sarah about three things, two of which you illustrated beautifully.

"If someone grabs you-- it is okay to yell, kick, scratch bite and make noise! Tell everyone you meet that you have been taken and where your home is.

"Just because someone might take you does not mean you cannot trust other people to help you get back home.

"Do not believe anything a person may say about your family not caring about you not wanting you or forgetting you. Those are lies!

"Your family will never stop loving you and they will search for you. People want to help bring you home.

"Thank you for caring.

"Barbara Pryor – Sarah's Mom"

We received an answer from Bill which read, "I hope God speeds Sarah's return." —Bill Keane and the Family Circus

February, 1986

ON THURSDAY, February 6, 1986, media reports stated:

> "The Middlesex's District Attorney's Office returned a Roxbury, MA woman to Boston from Puerto Rico. After telling various stories about what happened to Sarah, 26-year-old Laura Hawkins told police she was with two men who grabbed Sarah from Concord Road in Wayland and later dumped her body in an incinerator at Columbia Point in Dorchester, MA. When the investigative team was unable to corroborate any of her stories, Ms. Hawkins was convicted of perjury and sentenced to jail."

Tom Reilly called saying that the news media had uncovered the Hawkins story and were ready to make it public. As District Attorney, he had asked for a news embargo to go into effect on Friday night until the investigators could verify if there was truth in her statements. A second call came from Steve Delinsky, the attorney Bradford School had hired on our behalf to help Andy and me navigate through difficult days being in the public eye. He advised me to go home and prepare Meg and Byron for what might be a sudden media explosion about Sarah.

I asked Carroll to meet me at the house before Byron and Meg's bus arrived to help me decide what I should tell them. At 3:00 p.m. they burst into the family room joking with each other, then noticed us. Byron asked, "Mom, what are you doing home so early from work?"

I began my rehearsed sentences: "We have hoped that Sarah's story was going to turn out well. Now it is not looking so hopeful."

Meg yelled, "I hate it when you are not hopeful," and ran up the stairs and slammed her bedroom door.

Then on Sunday, February 9, 1986, *The Boston Herald* informed the DA's office Sunday evening that they would no longer honor the news embargo and would run the story Monday morning. The newspaper devoted the first dozen pages in their February 10, 1986 morning edition to pictures of Sarah and articles including speculations about Laura Hawkins.

I wrote a stern letter to the editor describing the havoc created by reporting that described the supposed rape of a child when that had never been established. Unforgivably those reports were then heard by young classmates and friends of Sarah's. Crisis management teams were sent to the school to talk with parents and children about topics foreign to their innocence. I decided to no longer cooperate with the *Herald*. Sometime later I received a terse response to my letter, with no apology, but the excuse, "We reported rape because we thought she was dead."

At 7:00 a.m. on *News Headline Radio* on Monday, February 10, 1986, they stated:

"According to the cover story in today's *Boston Herald*, based on an informant's story, Sarah Pryor, missing from Wayland, was kidnapped, raped, and murdered."

Byron and I were downstairs in the kitchen. I stood at the stove as he ate his cereal and listened to the radio before leaving for school. When he heard the jolting news about his sister, Byron stopped eating; set his spoon down, unable to continue.

"Mom,:" he said, "I'm sick in my stomach."

Among the other media announcements, according to the *Middlesex News*, also on Monday, February 10, 1986:

"Police search Columbia Point in Dorchester after 26-year-old Laura Hawkins of Roxbury, a Combat Zone dancer, told police she was with two men who dumped Sarah Pryor's body in incinerators there. Police search Columbia Point in Dorchester. A search turns up nothing."

Andy and I met with the investigators about Laura Hawkins. When they were unable to substantiate any truth in what she had alleged they proceeded to a perjury charge. I was confused and angry. Why would someone make up horrible lies about our Sarah? I raised my hand to ask a question although I was afraid to hear the answer.

"Is it possible that we may never know what happened to Sarah?" I asked the police.

"Yes, it is possible," someone on the team answered.

"Is it *probable* that we will never know?"

The quick response, "Yes."

It was at that moment I began to try and adjust my expectations to be more realistic, all the while I was determined to hold on to hope in some part of me.

Knowing the investigations team couldn't corroborate any of her accusations, Laura Hawkins admitted to "making it all up." She was convicted of perjury for the false tale that Sarah's raped body was buried in a Columbia Point apartment building. She was sentenced to serve what I thought was very little time for a horrible lie.

Meanwhile at home, our two teenagers grieved in different ways. Byron chose not to talk about Sarah's fate. Meg didn't want to see anything in my behavior that hinted that Sarah was not alive. I said little about the investigation to Meg, waiting for her to give me clues if she wanted information. Meg was forced to let down her guard as the Laura Hawkins false testimony deeply affected her. Going into Meg's bedroom one morning to awaken her, I said my daily greeting, "Good morning sweetheart, it's time get up." She usually rose with a few grumbles and began dressing for school. This day was different.

"Mommy," she said, in a voice of a young child, "will you come and sit with me, hold my hand, please."

This isn't the tough junior varsity lacrosse team goalie, all padded for battle. My daughter is frightened, I thought.

She began crying, saying, "Mommy, I'm so scared."

Not knowing exactly what was coming, I reassured her she could tell me. Again, she said, "Mommy, Mommy." Suddenly I realized she was afraid to ask me a question because she knew I would answer truthfully. I prayed silently, *Help me to know what she can handle.* Finally, Meg asked, "Do the investigators think she isn't coming back?" That was the question she most dreaded.

Holding her, my arms wrapped around her, I answered as gently as I could, "Yes, sweetheart, they think she isn't coming back."

These words jolted her like an electric shock. She screamed. I heard Byron's footsteps on the stairs, racing to see what had happened to his sister. He stopped when I told him that we were okay. She had become as limp as a rag doll in my arms. We sat emotionally spent, but somehow better, beginning to weather this latest storm.

Meg had nothing more to say but started getting ready for school. When I came into her bedroom the next morning I found her curled in bed with Sarah's blond doll in one hand, and the small cross in the other. I gazed at my brave daughter, thinking, *My darling girl, what a badge of courage you are earning.*

It was a Saturday—February 22, 1986.

The next Friday, on February 28th—I don't remember if it was my idea or Meg's—we got out of town to escape New England's cold winter and the disturbing Laura Hawkins news coverage. Meg's spring break seemed the perfect time to head to Disneyland. I bought airplane tickets for us to fly to the Magic Kingdom with her friend Cammy. Andy drove us to the airport then returned home to take care of the house with Byron while we were away.

The weather was picture perfect with a sky the most beautiful robin's egg blue and the temperature a sunny 75 degrees when we arrived at the park. The girls were eager to ride the rides and capture every moment of their vacation. I was content to sit on a bench, enjoying the sunshine, reading a book, watching families enjoying the World of Disney. I insisted that the two check in with me at regular intervals in the mornings and in the afternoons after we ate lunch together. I realized that I was fighting a nagging fear, *What if they were abducted while out of sight?*

But they were compliant, arriving without fail as they promised.

Mind wandering, I sat looking at the vacationing people when suddenly I saw Sarah walking toward me. *What joy! Sarah is here! She comes running towards me with a big smile, her arms outstretched ready to hug me in a long-awaited embrace* . . . An instant later I returned to the real world and sighed a sigh of disappointment. Then there was a Monarch butterfly fluttering near my left arm. Sitting still, not daring to move, I watched it settle on my outstretched arm. I spoke softly, "Hello, Sarah," and it took flight.

That evening we stood in the middle of Main Street where vacationers paid little attention to us. Cammy watched as Meg and I grasped two newly purchased balloons. The blue balloon was for baby Drew, my nephew, who had died shortly after his birth two years ago. The yellow balloon was for his cousin, Sarah, one of eleven cousins he would never know. Meg tenderly released the blue balloon saying, "This is for you, Drew."

I gently let go of the yellow balloon and said, "This one is for you, Sweetie. I wish you were here with us."

We watched the two balloons take flight and gain altitude—up, up, up, as we stood with our arms around each other, tears flowing, staring into space, not wanting to lose sight of the balloons. Shielding our eyes from the sun we kept the balloons in sight for ten minutes, wondering if anyone noticed. I smiled as I thought of the balloons shining as brightly as stars that night.

[5] SILENCE IS NOT GOLDEN

March, 1986

MY SPIRIT WAS LIFTED reminding me that our family was not forgotten whenever I received an unexpected phone call or a note from a friend back in my hometown in Pennsylvania. Their love was sent to us in the midst of our chaotic lives telling us they shared our mournful emotions just as they had wished us happiness in our new lives when they had said their farewells less than a year ago.

Answering the phone one day I smiled to hear the sweet, soft voice of my friend Carol Stevenson. I told her she had made my day and we chuckled together. We exchanged the pleasantries of two friends catching up about our children and their lives, then she shifted to a more serious tone.

"Barbara," she said, "I have something to tell you and I don't want to." I heard sniffles—she was crying.

"Carol, it's okay, really, you can tell me anything."

"I have been in prayer daily talking with God about Sarah and pleading with Him to return her to your family. Today I was again begging Him, *Please, please bring Sarah home.*" Carol stopped talking. I waited, and then, "Barbara, this is the hard part," her voice sobbed, "I heard Him say clearly, *But Carol, Sarah is at home, she is with Me.* No, I said, no. *Yes, she is home with Me.* Barbara, I am so sorry to tell you."

Immediately I said, "My dear friend, thank you for being brave enough to tell me. Thank you." She did not see my tears flowing, nor hear anguish in my voice as I worked hard to use a comforting tone to end our conversation. After we said our good-byes I sat letting sadness engulf me, still processing what Carol had shared. I gave myself permission to let time pass and to think about it later, but I would never forget my loving friend's call.

April, 1986

A NEW FRIEND, Mary Malcomson, invited me to a birthday celebration for her daughter Cathy on April 13, 1986. Family and friends gathered to celebrate her seventeenth birthday but there was no cake, no ice cream, no presents, and no Cathy. In August, two months before Sarah went missing, Mary reported her 16-year-old daughter failed to return from her job at a nursing home in her hometown of Hudson (about 12 miles from Wayland).

Mary phoned me soon after Sarah was missing, offering comfort.

We became friends walking a similar journey. Mary Malcolmson told me that the local police department had said her Cathy was likely a runaway and would return home. So on April 13, 1986, Mary was determined to honor Cathy's birthday. We learned later that the Middlesex District Attorney's office suspected the same serial perpetrator might have taken both Cathy and Sarah.

At Cathy's birthday celebration, Mary thanked people for what they had done to help her while she was waiting for Cathy's return. She asked me how I was doing—even if we both cried! She gave me a simple touch or hug—no words were necessary. She dropped a note in the mail, and even if she didn't know it, sometimes it gave me the strength to face the next hour. Mary told me she was thinking of Sarah or praying for her, that she had not forgotten her. Mary shared her frustration and anger that this could happen.

Silence is not golden. If you don't mention our child for fear you will upset us, we are likely to misinterpret your silence and suspect your failure to acknowledge our children. We think you don't care.

Thank you, Mary—for risking, for being willing to show me your love.

May, 1986

ON A PROMISING spring day bright with sunshine, perfect for music in the outdoors, Claypit Hill Elementary School was honoring Sarah by planting a dogwood tree. Our family arrived while students helped the custodian arrange folding chairs and music stands for the celebration. A piano was rolled out into the circular drive and set to rest next to the flagpole. The children's voices rang with laughter in spite of a sudden gentle spring shower. When the rain ended, the fourth and fifth grade band members took their places circling the music teacher.

The audience said the Pledge of Allegiance, then the band played "America" and "Yankee Doodle" and "To Every Season." As I looked at the smiling children I thought they seemed happy singing and thinking about their missing classmate. For a moment I searched for Sarah's face—it should have been near the back, where all the tall kids stood. I thought I heard her voice, singing enthusiastically, loudly, and so off-key! As I absentmindedly searched for her face, I heard the lyrics more clearly:

To every season, turn, turn, turn,

There is a reason, turn, turn, turn

A time to be born and a time to die

Suddenly, I felt sorrow fill me as I pleaded silently, *Please don't let me cry*. Smiling my brightest pretend smile, tears streaming down my face—

. . . turn, turn, turn

A time to weep and a time to laugh

A time to mourn and a time to dance

A student in the first row said to the friend beside her, "Mrs. Pryor's crying," but I maintained my wobbly smile.

June, 1986

"Love, like the ocean, is vast and forever and sorrow but a shadow that is cast upon the sea. May the forever of love soon bear the grief of this hour away from your heart."

—(Author unknown)

HOW MANY TIMES have I written the above quotation in notes of sympathy to those who are grieving? From my early childhood days when family vacations—including trips to Cape May, New Jersey—I have always loved the ocean, the sound of the ocean constant, as the waves beat the rhythm of eternity. Our family had always looked forward to the Pryor summer vacation traveling to Rehoboth Beach, Delaware, where we rented a beach house for a sun and fun week. We tried to imagine how we could vacation this June without Sarah.

Now enjoying the warmth of the sandy beach, I looked out at the ocean that seemed without limit and thought how I had mailed notes to hearts that grieved the loss of someone in their lives. I thought of caring cards of encouragement I had received in the last six months often from people I did not know. Why was I feeling no comfort today?

Sarah was five years old when we were last at the beach. She embraced the ocean, running into it wearing her goggles and water wings; jumping, falling, righting herself for another adventure. She welcomed the waves, her energy a good match to the boundless wit of the ocean. Suddenly I realized Meg was 10, the age her sister Sarah should have been that day.

I gazed out at the horizon and saw endlessness not just of the ocean, but in my heart and I thought, *It is unfair.*

Sarah should be here with us. I could hear her voice, full of life and love, exclaiming, "I can't wait to go back to the beach!"

And I wondered why the grief of that hour felt like it was vast and forever.

IN JUNE, a Father's Day card came from Meg to Andy along with a *Directory of Missing and Abducted Children, Fifth Edition*, printed by Ford Motor Company in conjunction with Child Find, Inc. It held Sarah's debut—Sarah Elizabeth Pryor, File Number 3504-S found on page 28. Hers was one of 527 names and pictures of parental abduction, stranger abduction, or runaway cases. I looked at her page and wondered, *Why? In a nation that has support groups to Save the Seals, Save the Whales, Save The Redwoods, why is there no group to save our most important resource, our children? What are the priorities of a nation where we rally to protect animals and trees and fail to see our children who go missing? Don't our children have the right to play outside of their homes and be safe?*

I have thought, as I imagine other parents of missing children have wondered, what could I have done differently while training my child. Maybe I shouldn't have worked so hard on teaching her to be brave, showing her she could trust, telling her not to be afraid. I did what I thought every parent should do, foster responsibility and independence. She should have been able to come home from an after-school walk on a beautiful fall day. How hard I worked helping her to be brave, to be confident. How much patience it took. *For what purpose?*

Why?

July, 1986

ANDY DROVE THE FAMILY to Boston's Logan Airport on that hot Fourth of July. Byron and Meg were eager to return to their Summer's Best Two Weeks camp near Somerset, PA. They had been campers every year and Sarah had been old enough to be with them at camp for the first time the summer of 1985.

That year Pittsburgh friends agreed to collect Byron and Meg and deliver them to camp. I watched their plane take off for Pittsburgh until it disappeared into clouds and sighed, sitting for a moment in the terminal letting sadness overcome me. Realizing that our house would be noticeably quiet without children, I said, "Andy, let's not go home to an empty house. Let's walk and enjoy the streets of Boston." We parked at Boston Harbor and people watched, as our path took us among the throngs enjoying the holiday.

Later in the week the Camp Director, our friend Jim Welch, phoned to tell us his concern for Meg and Byron. He confided that most campers seemed uncomfortable not knowing what to say about Sarah, afraid to make a hurtful comment, so it seemed to them best not to say anything. Jim invited campers to a fireside chat with Meg and Byron. He said a few words, then gave an invitation to campers for questions or comments. The plan worked to ease the awkwardness and bring comfort to our children.

Meg wrote from camp:

> "Dear Mom,
>
> "A friend is trying to help me give God the control, and not to hang on to my wants. It's hard for me to do, but I am trying. I want to, but I feel like I'm

betraying Sarah, or that, if I give God control, it means He can do what He wants, and He could let her die. Well, I'm trying. Everyone has been so helpful and loving, and willing to be there. Byron and I are speaking at the campfire service on Sunday night. I pray that God will give us the words.

"There's a little girl in cabin 2 who reminds me of Sarah at age 7 or 8. She even talks with her r's like w's. It's very hard for me to see her, but in a way, it's like a reminder of happy times! You know what I mean? I've done a lot of crying, and I imagine I'll do a lot more. It's comforting to have so many loving people around. Their hugs and loving, encouraging words are like those of God.

"Love, Meg"

A PHONE CALL came to me at work from Byron late Wednesday afternoon. "Mom, the mother of the 19-year-old girl missing since Monday night just called. Someone at a local TV station gave her our phone number. She'd really like to talk to you. I think it's important to call her."

I assured him I would do it, dialing immediately after I thanked him for the call. I didn't know what I'd say but I would help if I could. I wondered if the mother was in shock. Had she slept since Monday? Had she eaten? Were neighbors and friends helping her? How were her husband and her other children managing?

When Paula Danforth answered I introduced myself. She thanked me for calling and began describing the events that had drastically changed their lives. Her daughter,

Paula, usually drove to the nursing home where she worked, but her dad and her boyfriend had been repairing her car and it wasn't ready when she called at 9:00 p.m. to be picked up after work. Paula said she would walk the two miles to her boyfriend's apartment, but she had not arrived.

I asked, "Are you able to sleep?"

"Yes, I slept a bit last night."

"Are you eating?"

"I'm trying to."

"That's good," I said. "Maybe I can share with you some things that helped me. I found I had to let people help. You need your strength and people want to be useful. Somehow it helps them. We had neighbors, friends, and even people we didn't know arrive to take our laundry and even our garbage away. Another crew answered our phones and talked to the media. Batches of food arrived. Our freezer bulged with casseroles. Accept the help. But what you really have to concentrate on is eating and sleeping. Let people help you. Keep a notebook of every call that comes in. Note the time, the person calling, and the nature of the call. If it's a collect call, ask the operator what number is calling before accepting."

I talked with her about what had helped us while working with the media. We issued a press statement every day. We were frightened by the media at first but we received very good advice about how much we needed them. They could get Sarah's story in front of as many people as possible in hopes of finding her. For the most part members of the media cared. The press statements we issued helped us avoid question-and-answer press conferences because we realized we could not think clearly when we were dealing with our raw emotions.

Then I said, "Your husband and Paula's boyfriend must be upset. I hope they aren't thinking, *If only we had fixed the car earlier.* No one needs added guilt."

Paula was silent for a moment and then said, "Barbara, my husband's brother disappeared seven years ago and hasn't been seen since."

"I'm so sorry, you and your husband must be hurting beyond belief."

We were interrupted by another call on her line and we said a quick goodbye. The next day when I came in the front door after work Andy startled me by saying, "Sit down." I fell into a chair. "They have found a murdered body. They believe it to be Paula's daughter." I sat trying to take in the terrible news, then got up and headed to the phone. I knew Paula's mother wouldn't be able to come to the phone, but I would leave a message for the family.

When a young male voice answered I identified myself. "This is Barbara Pryor calling and I'd like to leave a message for Paula's mom. Please tell her the Pryor Family sends their love to your family." His voice broke, and I asked, "Is this her brother?"

"Yes," he sobbed.

"We love you," I said. "Goodbye for now."

Six days after Paula's burial I called again to find out how another hurting mom was managing. I would begin checking in on them on a weekly basis.

[6] AMAZED &

GRATEFUL

"A Secret Service agent calls police after spotting a girl resembling Sarah Pryor in a station wagon near Bourne Beach. Police search all night before finding a Millis girl who they say is the *spitting image* of Sarah."

—*Boston Herald*, August 7, 1986

August, 1986

ONE SUMMER EVENING, I answered the phone to the voice of Marty Sender, one of our favorite TV reporters. "Do you know about the search on the Cape for Sarah? The police are following a lead. A girl who resembled Sarah was seen on the beach today with a family." I told her I had not heard but I thanked him for the heads-up, alerted my family, and sat thinking: *The roller coaster ride continued, we had grown almost accustomed to leads for a look-alike girl,* I thought. *Thankfully, this is much better than searches for Sarah's remains.* I knew worrying all night would not determine the outcome. After saying good night to my family, I prayed, and slept peacefully.

Early the next morning, Chief Galvin called to say that investigators had located a family's van in the town of Bourne at 4:00 a.m., a block from Sarah Street! A vacationing criminal justice agent had spotted the Sarah look-alike with a family of four on the beach. The girl was markedly off by herself, not relating to the rest of the family. He followed them to their car, phoned in the license plate, and learned that the out-of-state dentist had only two very young children. Clearly the pre-teen was not theirs. That finding intensified the search. When the midwestern dentist was located, it turned out that the girl was a niece from a Boston suburb vacationing with them. She was a "spitting-image of Sarah," he reported. The father, apparently torn from his bed at the early morning hour, expressed his amazement at the extreme measures the police took to find and assure the safety of a missing child.

I was amazed and grateful as well.

A FAMILY FRIEND, the Reverend David Jones, told Fred Rogers of "Mr. Roger's Neighborhood" about Sarah. The two ordained ministers were close friends. Byron, Meg, and Sarah had been loyal viewers of the television show. David phoned our home to tell us Fred asked for a telephone conversation with the family. A week later, I answered the phone to hear the familiar voice of Mr. Rogers.

"How are you doing, Barbara?" he asked. Unhurriedly, he chatted, concerned about how I was doing, listening, and telling me he often thought of our family.

I handed the phone to Andy to continue the conversation. Byron burst through the front door with several of his basketball teammates. Meg silenced their raucous laughter and teasing with her command, "Be quiet, you guys. Dad's on the phone with Mr. Rogers!" Byron's status grew among his peers as they recounted their fond memories of Mr. Rogers. Meg was next to talk, saying, "I'm lucky, Mr. Rogers, I grew up with you in my childhood and I was watching you all over again, with Sarah."

I smiled as I heard my son now on the line. "So, how are you doing, Mr. Rogers?" Byron finished the conversation by asking Mr. Rogers to send a photo for the Wayland High School locker room, with the inscription, "To the Wayland team. Good luck at states."

Long after the conversation that day, we had a kind new friend. Mr. Rogers, you were special to us. We will not forget your caring heart.

THAT AUGUST, Andy wrote in his journal:

> "When the police receive what they consider a valid tip about Sarah's whereabouts, the family is in turmoil as hope stirs up. There have been dozens of tips. I tend to be somewhat of a reserved individual, but I feel things deeply. I'm on an emotional roller coaster. I can't verbalize how it has changed me. We have tried to put our lives back into some semblance of order."

September, 1986

WHEN WE MOVED into our new home, Sarah was delighted to have a room all of her own. Every night she climbed up into her four-poster double bed so glad to leave her shared room with her sister. Stuffed animals and pillows in quilted shams adorned her new bed. A lamp and her light-up cross sat on the end table. After Sarah took her walk that day in October and never returned home, Meg and Byron insisted that Sarah's room stay exactly as it was the last day she left the house.

We wrapped Christmas gifts for her, placing them under the decorated tree with our gifts. At the end of December, the tree was dragged outside, and Sarah's Christmas gifts were added to the stuffed animals on her bed. The next month *birthday* presents crowded the collection. I could not bring myself to go into her bedroom and often walked quickly past the open door, unwilling to see what looked frozen in time—a painful reminder that she was out there, somewhere.

A year later in September, I realized that the clothes in Sarah's closet and her dresser would no longer fit her, should she return. I didn't want to look at the clothes, let alone give them away. I was avoiding a painful chore, remembering how sad Sarah had been as grew taller, in a matter of months no longer fitting into her clothes. She would cry and plead, "Please don't give my favorite clothes away, Mommy. I love them." I told her the clothes would make other little girls happy. My advice was unheeded, she held fast, not wanting to let go.

I wondered, *Why did Sarah not want to let go of her clothes?* I sat on her bedroom floor as tears filled my eyes missing her so much.

Bright sunlight beamed through the window to help me dry my tears. I breathed a sigh of relief knowing my sister would help me with this difficult job. Carroll came quickly and together we sorted, packed, and brought the things to a local thrift shop, then treated ourselves to a lunch.

BARBARA SMITH PRYOR

PART TWO:
ANGELS & DEMONS

[7] DAFFODILS

AND ROSES

October 9, 1986

WITHIN SIX MONTHS the Middlesex District
Attorney's Office had proposed a timeline
starting from the time Sarah left our home at
4:00 p.m. on October 9th, 1985. The timeline included
statements from people who provided information to the
Wayland Police Department about what they remembered
that seemed out of the ordinary—things like seeing a car,
a man or a girl. In a press conference Chief Gerry Galvin
had asked the public to provide any information and
promised that his department would follow every lead. A
year later, on October 9th, 1986, the investigative team
walked Andy and me along the route, while John McEvoy,

one of the Assistant District Attorneys, recounted the possible sightings. We made the Sarah journey in reverse, ending at the Wayland Police Station.

A woman land surveyor had her memory jogged by the continuing news about Sarah. She had noticed a girl on the sidewalk talking to someone in a parked vehicle several hundred feet from our house at 152 Concord Road. When she checked her records, it was October 9th, shortly after 4:00 p.m. The police suspected with the window rolled down the person asked the girl for directions (a stalker's known delay tactic).

Further down Sarah's path a man was reported standing beside his car with the hood up as though he was experiencing car trouble. The investigators suspected the man was waiting, allowing Sarah to pass without realizing she might be in danger until he could have the opportunity to grab her when there was a lull in the busy traffic flow.

A man was reported at the corn field sitting on the hood of his car (similar to the previous sighting). A woman and her mother traveling south on Route 126 spotted the man who seemed out of place and somewhat frightening to them. They did not see Sarah, only the man lounging on the hood. Months later, a television (WBZ) news reporter, Charlie Austin, interviewed and photographed Sarah's alleged abductor when he was incarcerated in Norfolk, Massachusetts. The woman turned on her TV to hear, "Stay tuned for the latest in the Sarah Pryor Investigation." She sat in shock as she realized she recognized the man who had been sitting on the hood of his car that day at the cornfield. After her call to the Wayland police she was interviewed and pronounced a reliable witness.

Another woman and her 10-year-old son were riding bikes on the path almost to the northern border of Wayland. She noticed a man lurking on the path whom she later reported looked suspicious, asking herself, "What was he doing on the path?" She watched her son intently as he rode safely past the man. Investigators showed her composite pictures of men including Sarah's alleged abductor. The women said she was so focused on her son and his safety she could not identify the man, but her son thought he recognized the man.

A man and his teen age son were traveling south on Route 126, near the Wayland/Lincoln border. The dad noticed a parked car by the side of the road, commenting that the car was the same model and year as a relative's. He saw a girl walking, joking with his son, "There is a pretty girl for you." Then he added, "She looks younger than I thought." They made a turn off the road to deliver a package to his brother's house and returned to route 126, heading north on their return trip. The car and the girl were gone. Police investigators later drove the distance from the spot from where he noticed the car and the girl, the delivery, and the return to the Route 126 sighting. It took less than 20 minutes. They believe this was when Sarah was abducted. The estimated complete time taken for stalking and abduction was approximately one hour and 10 minutes as illustrated by the investigator's time line.

November 1986

"After Cal died it was just about going forward in those days one step, one step—not falling down into myself. I didn't think about changing my life—my life had already been changed. I just had to get through it."

—Anne Patchett, *Commonwealth*

THESE WORDS DESCRIBED what Andy, Meg, Byron, and I often felt after Sarah was missing. We plodded through day-by-day, trying to adjust to a new world, one that was fragile and tenuous, and left us vulnerable to what would happen next. A year after Sarah was abducted Andy, Byron and I sat in family counseling without Meg, as she preferred individual counseling. We were in the grief counselor's office for a one-time meeting. I looked at the pleasant décor, thinking the tidy office contrasted to our lives which seemed in constant disarray as months dragged on without answers. The psychologist asked Byron, "Where is Sarah to you?"

After a long pause Byron said, "I see Sarah that day in October heading out for her walk as I mowed the grass in the backyard and waved good-bye. She had walked to a cornfield the day before and was proud, saying she hoped to walk farther in exploring her new neighborhood. I see her leaving for her walk and then I see her with God." Byron paused, then said, "Everything else is too hard to imagine."

Poetry

ONE OF THE ways our family dealt with and communicated the emptiness in our lives without Sarah was by writing poetry. We wrote privately, later offering our works to each other. Here are poems by Byron and Meg:

THE DAFFODIL

From Byron to Sarah, wherever she may be, May, 1986

I once watched a daffodil as it grew from a bulb.

As it grew, it got larger and larger.

With every day, it became stronger and wiser.

It possessed a simple beauty that is so very rare.

This daffodil taught me so much;

It taught me of love and the beauty of innocence.

It began to bloom into the most enthralling yellow.

It was the blazing yellow of the setting sun.

Standing so majestically on its stalk,

I watched in horror as this once gorgeous creature was
cut down.

I cried; was enraged because the daffodil was no more.

Then I realized, the daffodil wasn't mine to have.

I could only gaze at it, admire it, and learn from it

while it was yet alive.

A SISTER'S LAMENT

Meg Pryor, October, 1986

As I lie here in my lonely room, my thoughts drift back to
you, as they often do.

I miss you so much, I physically ache.

I hurt so much it scares me.

If only I could take back the wrongs

And make them right. They all seem so silly now.

Why did I pull away from you

When I really wanted to get closer?

How could I hurt you with my unkind words

When I knew they could cut like knives?

And why couldn't I tell you

How much I love you,

And how special you are to me?

I could never purposely hurt you

In fact I wanted to shield you

From all the pain in the world.

But I couldn't protect you. No one could.

And now you're gone, and I miss you.

And I hate myself. I want to see you again.

To hear your voice, your laughter,

To tell you I love you.

You mean the world to me

And I know that the pain won't end;

Not until I'm with you

And I can read you this, and hug you, hold you tight.

And never let you go again.

Some Notes of Comfort

"My heart goes out to you two, as it so
often has since your daughter Sarah (was

missing). Kitty and I can only imagine the anguish you have endured and the strength you have had to find. The State Police Missing Persons unit ... continues to participate in the investigation of your daughter's case, working with both the Wayland Police and the Middlesex County District Attorney's Office. I continue to share your hope that she will be found and restored to her family. Let me know if there is anything I can do to end or alleviate your ordeal."

—Michael S. Dukakis

Governor of the Commonwealth of Massachusetts

"Let me voice my deepest sympathy for the tragedy that you have endured. The strength you have shown in what must be the most painful experience of your life is to be commended."

—Richard G. Lugar

U.S. Senator, Indiana

"I am praying with you that your story will have a happy ending."

—Robert H. Michel

U.S. Republican Leader 18th District, Illinois

"US Department of Education Secretary, William Bennett, and I were very grieved to hear about Sarah, and angered as you are, that this unexplained abduction could have occurred."

—Peter R. Greer

Deputy/Under Secretary, US Department of Education

"I was sorry to learn that the very worst thing that could happen has visited your family. The abduction of your darling daughter goes beyond the point of heartbreak. We are all so very helpless in these situations."

—Richard A. Gephardt

Former Minority-Whip, U.S. House of Representatives and classmate, and friend of Barbara. (We served together on the Student Senate at Northwestern University, Evanston, Illinois.)

"I think of you often especially so this spring when my daffodils bloomed for Sarah. I haven't given up hope but knowing you and this event has changed my life. It changes the way I deal with children. I am no longer impatient with my six-year-old neighbor and I watch him all the way home though he lives just next door. I once said to Andy that I feel America was no longer my country and my hope was to settle in some little village in Scotland or Ireland where morality might be different. But Andy said we had the greatest country in the world, and convinced me, in some ways, that this was true. The freedom, the possibilities are there—yet I continue to be disillusioned by many things. Perhaps, *We live in the best of times, the worst of times.* (Dickens)"

—Louise McClenathan

Pittsburgh friend

We received two notes from the 4 and 6-year-old sons of our friends, the Tolhursts, who had moved to Ohio from our community in Pennsylvania:

"I remember when Sarah visited us and we played hide and seek and played the piano. I feel sad about Sarah being gone. Maybe she will turn up."

—Love, Andrew

"I feel super sad."

—Love, Ryan.

Year End 1986

AND BY YEAR'S end this neatly printed prayer letter
came to us from the 12-year-old daughter of our friends,
Carol and John Stevenson:

> "This is a prayer I made up. It's sorta
> dumb, But I hope you like it.
>
> Dear Father in Heaven: Sarah's lost.
> Please, wherever Sarah is, please watch
> over her. You're the only one that knows
> where Sarah is. Please let her be found
> unharmed and not hurt. Let her find food
> to eat and let her have shelter. Whoever has
> her, please don't let him or her harm Sarah.
> Thanks for everything. Love ya always
> amen. Xo
>
> —Beth Ann Stevenson (age 12)
>
> That's close to my prayer I say going to bed
> xo

And from a new-found friend in Massachusetts:

> "This poem is for you and for your
> wonderful strength which you have given
> me since we first met. I wrote love letters
> to my family and continue to pass on

Sarah's example about living life like a nine-year-old."

—Love, J. Spur

You are a Garden

and Sarah is Your Prize Rose

You Created the Beauty of the Rose

and Even When It was Taken Away

You Always Gave Us a Chance to

See the Beauty

Thru Your Eyes

You Could Create Such a

Beautiful Image of Love

to Everyone You Touched

With the Memory of Your Rose

Although Some Would See the Thorns

You Would Always Lead Them

Back to the Color

Or the Beauty of the Petals

Yet We Never Saw the Rose

the Fragrance Lingers

and Helps Us to Grow

In Knowing the Rose.

[8] OUR STORIES

March 1987

BABS MURPHY'S STORY was told to me by the minister who officiated at the funeral of her youngest child. She had lost two children to cystic fibrosis, most recently Bruce, age 19, on March 22, 1987. The eulogy praised his parents for encouraging their son's zest for living his short life. Bruce was a toddler when his older sister died at the age of seven.

When I heard this family's story, I couldn't imagine parents living day-after-day knowing what was inevitable. My loss seemed to be smaller, somehow less terrible. I thought about their suffering as I opened the desk drawer where I kept my supplies. Taking out pen, flowered stationary, envelopes, and stamps, I began writing a note to this mother I hadn't met. I recalled with tenderness the notes that had come to me after Sarah was missing and how they had helped me get through each day. Envelopes were simply addressed, "The Pryor's c/o the Wayland Police Department." The messages were similar—"I'm sorry and I care." I learned a valuable lesson—to reach out to those I didn't know. On this day in March, I wrote "I am thinking of you today as I have every day since I heard of the sad loss to death of your son Bruce. Please know that I care about you and your family. I send you thoughts, prayers, and love." I mailed my message not expecting to hear from Babs. But the story was to take an unexpected turn: I was to receive a beautiful gift in return.

Babs told me her story:

"The first time I had to deal with the death of a child, I was consumed with talking about it. A doctor had warned me when Bruce died that I was likely to feel a different void. For nineteen years I'd had a responsible and demanding job dedicated to caring for Bruce. It occupied my time, energy and thoughts. The responsibility was gone, leaving a void, a deep hole in my heart. My husband had his Monday-through-Friday routine. Alone at home my mind took over like a videotape looping over and over, replaying scenes—the doctors, what they said, what they did, and the final moments with our son, our helplessness, our hopelessness. The stream of consciousness seemed unrelenting. There was no off switch. I was restless. When I awoke I wished his dying was something in a dream. I wondered about the strangest things, "Where were his shoes?" And I obsessed about details that didn't matter. I had no control over them.

Traveling was usually a good distraction for me; getting away had been an effective coping mechanism. I suspected it wouldn't help me this time because my head was still playing the tapes. Nevertheless, when my husband suggested touring the Carolinas I agreed because I thought it might help him to cope.

"We left Massachusetts heading south, endless thoughts spinning in my head. Within five days my numbness lessened, turning into agitation. I yearned for my home, my familiar kitchen, and my friends. Yet I dreaded going home, to see Bruce's room with all that reminded me of him.

"On the return trip through Maryland in early April, I heard Boston mentioned on the car radio, snapping me out of my silence, prompting me to say aloud, 'This is going to sound strange, but I know I'm going to hear from Barbara Pryor.' My husband looked at me inquisitively, silently wondering, I'm sure, if this startlingly irrational statement might be still another phenomenon of the grieving process. He acknowledged my departure from reality with appropriate and innocuous remarks like, 'Oh,' and 'Hmm.'

"Arriving home on my birthday, April 3rd, I walked into the house with mixed feelings. I was eager to hug our oldest son, Jim who had tended the house and collected our mail. Reality crept in. We were back, nothing had changed. Bruce's prized possessions waited silently, undisturbed in a ghostly permanent stillness. I walked from the beautiful flowers in the living room into the kitchen thinking, *I'm back.*

"Time marches on unrelentingly without him. I opened a kitchen cabinet to take out the box of tea bags. There staring at me was the arsenal of pills that Bruce had been prescribed—60-70 pills a day for all those years. And what did it matter? It didn't do him any good. I was mad at the pills and threw the whole supply away—attacking them, throwing them into a garbage bag. My body physically, mentally, and emotionally was depleted.

"I sat down to read the mail which Jim had arranged in neat stacks. With my cup of freshly brewed tea nearby, I picked up the bundle to see the first envelope I opened on the top of the stack was from Barbara Pryor—this woman I had never met. How did she live life, not knowing what had happened to her Sarah? My Bruce had been deeply moved by the loss of Sarah, talking openly and often about Sarah. He had her missing person picture hanging in his room from shortly after she was missing.

"This spring day, my birthday, I sat and read Barbara's note. Laying it down on the table next to my cup of tea I knew what I would do. An hour later, I arrived on the Pryor's doorstep with a potted plant in my hands, rang the doorbell and introduced myself.

"Hello, my name is Babs Murphy, I just read your note. *Thank you.*"

After that first meeting, Babs and I met twice a month for breakfast at Mel's the local Wayland diner. Two friends, two moms brought together in sorrow, peace, and love. We treasured the consolation of our new friendship and found more than mutual comfort as we shared our lives, struggles, and much laughter, with gratitude that our children had brought us together. Now, writing our stories, I thought about Babs' son, Jim, hoping he still lived in Wayland. I was delighted to find an address for him and wrote him a note. Here is his gracious reply:

"Dear Barbara:

"It was great to hear from you. I remember the friendship and mutual support that grew between the two of you. I remember Sarah. I sat with my mother at Sarah's funeral so many years ago. Since you have moved back to PA you may not know that unfortunately my dad, Chuck, passed away in April of 2012 and Mom in April of 2014. Hope all is going well with you.

"Take Care,

"Jim"

THAT SAME MONTH (March, 1987) our younger brother Stephen phoned to say he needed help with Mom. Her new psychiatrist had not believed Mom was bi-polar and had taken her off Lithium. He never returned Stephen's frantic calls, and Mom crashed. Carroll rushed to Pittsburgh, got her hospitalized and called to tell me of the situation. I booked a flight and went to her room as soon as I arrived at the hospital.

I barely recognized her. She was sitting in a chair, bent over, wringing her hands and looking helpless. Taking a chair next to her, holding her hand, I spoke gently saying I had come from Boston to spend a few hours with her. She barely acknowledged me, still wringing her hands repeating, "I don't know what I am supposed to do." Taking a deep breath, I gathered courage.

"Mom, you need to listen to me. I know you don't want to go on right now. But I have to tell you, if you don't want to go on, will you please do it for me? I cannot take another loss now, Mom. Please do it for me."

I sat a long time with her in silence, and offered a parting plea, "I hope you understand, Mom. Please do it for me." I returned on a same-day flight back to Boston. My heart told me Mom would honor my plea. After Mom was prescribed Lithium and back to her new normal, Carroll visited assisted living facilities, finding a perfect spot in Concord at the Rivercrest Deaconess Residence (assisted living facility), in Concord, Massachusetts, near Mom's home and easily accessible to mine as it was near Carroll and Bob's home and 20 minutes from my place. I was thankful for a new beginning for "Grandma Peg" as we called my mom, in spite of the frightening circumstances that brought her to us. We were pleased to have her near our families, especially with six of her grandchildren.

Before we moved to Massachusetts, my mother lived with our family in McMurray, Pennsylvania. Grandma Peg was a devoted nanny for Sarah while Andy and I were at work. One hectic day I answered the phone to hear my mother's cheerful voice:

"Sorry to interrupt you dear. Sarah asked me to sing 'Rock-a Bye-Baby,' but I didn't have the right words. Please sing a few lines for me."

Astonished, I replied, "Mom, I'm a little busy here." She persisted in an imploring way. I began to sing softly, somewhat embarrassed that a co-worker might hear me:

"Rock-a-bye baby,

on the tree top.

When the wind blows,

the cradle will rock."

She interrupted, "So, that's the way it goes? I was singing the other song, 'Rock-a-Bye Your Baby with a Dixie Melody.' Sarah told me, 'Grandma, that's not how it goes.'"

When Sarah was three years-old the two headed out to the shopping mall. Once they finished their errands they walked hand-in-hand to the parking lot. Grandma had the car key ready to unlock the car door when Sarah spoke.

"Grandma, it's not your car." Looking more closely, Grandma saw it was not her car.

"Sarah," she asked, "How did you know the difference?"

Sarah responded, "That car had rust spots."

The twosome had fun to the exclusion of friends their own ages. I decided to enroll Sarah in a daycare program for a few days a week telling the pair the plan. I was driving home from work one late afternoon thinking about Sarah's first day at daycare. I greeted my mother, asking, "How did it go with Sarah today?"

"She wouldn't go," Mom replied.

"What do you mean?"

"Sarah wouldn't get into the car."

Impatiently, I said, "Mother, you're older, and I think smarter, you had six kids for heaven's sake. Why didn't you put her in the car?"

Her feeble answer: "She didn't want to go!"

Turning to Sarah I said, "I told you that you were going to have fun. You have to go tomorrow!"

The next day I came home, again asking, "How did it go?"

My mother repeated, "She would not go."

I turned to Sarah and said, "Sarah Elizabeth Pryor, what's going on?"

She said, "I'll show you."

She took my hand, led me to the car, ordering me, "Open the door."

When I opened the door, Sarah hopped into the back seat. She pointed to her feet saying, "Look. My feet don't touch the floor, I'm too little to go."

Now years later Mother was coping with the absence of her sweet Sarah, still missing. I knew Mother did not watch the news or read the newspaper. I understood her reluctance—she didn't want to hear the on-going news about the searches for Sarah. Instead Carroll brought Mother a weekly supply of large-print books from the Concord Library to satisfy her love of reading.

Saturdays were appointed my luncheon dates with Grandma Peg. I'd get her into the car, drive to a restaurant, help her inside, eat, help her back into the car and then back to her room. We'd sit and chat while I caught my breath before heading out to run my weekly errands. One Saturday she seemed to be insisting that I leave, and I wondered, *Why the hurry?* I said goodbye, hugged her, and went to the door. Turning around I spotted the reason for her dismissal. She was concentrating on her current book selection.

The most intimate conversations with my mom came when she was a passenger as I drove to our Saturday lunch dates or took a Sunday drive to admire New England scenery. She would not share her sadness about losing Sarah, the pain was too great. One Sunday drive we were enjoying the beauty of the day when Mom broke the silence with her mind's wanderings. I'd grown accustomed to these moments of intimacy, and fond of being privy to a conversation or her stream of consciousness. She looked away, seeming oblivious to me sitting beside her, and fixed her gaze out the window.

"Remember," she said, "I have a storage chest in the basement."

I waited, asking myself, *What did she mean?* I responded with a guess: "Are you eager to get your winter clothes from storage?"

Slowly she answered, "No, I just want someone to remember it after I'm gone."

I glanced at her and decided she was thinking aloud. "I'll remember, Mom."

I forced myself to remain absolutely silent. Moments passed and she continued, "Just because I don't talk about Sarah, doesn't mean I don't think of her every day." I waited knowing for certain she was not finished with sharing her thoughts. I was not disappointed, for then she said, "When I get to heaven I'll be so happy to see Sarah.

Oh, I want to see her again. Maybe she'll want me to sing to her, just the way I used to."

Mom insisted that her six kids celebrate with a party rather than stand around crying when it was time for her to leave this earth. Margaret White Smith wanted to live to the turn of the century 2000, to celebrate her 90th birthday on April 21ˢᵗ along with Queen Elizabeth. She had often quipped, "I'm not in a hurry to go, but when I go I want to go in a hurry." Mom got her wish, enjoyed a fun birthday celebration with her kids, and a month later died, three days after having a stroke. Carroll took care of the contents of Mother's mysterious treasure chest.

[9] MESSAGES FOR

SARAH

August 1987

A COLUMNIST FROM the *Chicago Tribune* wrote us a letter in August of 1987. Bob Greene began an article, "Every time I see a picture of the Berlin Wall, all I can think of is Sarah Pryor." A fellow journalist had sent him a picture of a mysterious message to Sarah on the high concrete barrier that divided East and West Germany. The message read, "Sarah Pryor, wherever you are, we love you. Missing 10/9/85, Whalen, MA, God loves you." The writing appeared in 1986, on the Berlin Wall clearly visible some ten feet up on the western side at the top of the wall, unreachable from the ground. The location must have been carefully chosen where search lights on the free side of the Wall would illuminate it at night. I wondered who could have been so bold, climbing a ladder to spray-paint the message in spite of danger if East German guards discovered the writer. The message spread a long way across the wall's rim. The painter must have had to move the ladder several times. I was grateful, and mystified.

From 1986 to 1989, numerous photos and notes came to us from strangers who had been blessed by reading the inscription. They were sent to the Wayland Police Department or to local newspapers and then forwarded to us.

Though the face of the Wall changed drastically over time, the message to our Sarah remained at Check Point Charlie for thousands of visitors to see over the span of three years. We never discovered the identity of the brave person who climbed so high to beam Sarah's message. My brother David and his wife were stationed in Germany for a three-year assignment. I wondered if the writer was inspired by my brother's article about Sarah's kidnapping, which had been published in *Stars and Stripes*.

When the Berlin Wall was dismantled in 1989, I had mixed feelings. I celebrated in my heart that German neighbors and families would be reunited again and began to have hope for sustained peace, yet, the message of love for my Sarah was no longer visible for the world to see.

Check Point Charlie at Berlin Wall 1986, with message to Sarah from unknown sympathizer.

WHEN I WAS longing for hopeful news about Sarah or when media stories speculating hard endings to her life appeared, I tried to think of experiences that could help me in my current distress. One thought came back about Byron in his freshmen year of high school in Pennsylvania. One evening I was in the bedroom having left him with Andy watching TV. From my sleep, I heard the deep voice of my tall son saying, "Mom, can I talk with you?" I sat up and realized that what was about to take place would be something different from ordinary conversations about dinner or his plans for the evening.

He sat down at the edge of my bed. "Mom, I have a friend at school. On Tuesday her Mom got sick. On Wednesday she was in the hospital. The next day she died."

I responded, "Oh, I am so sorry."

85

Silence for a moment, then, he continued, "I don't know what I'm supposed to do."

Confused, I asked, "What do you think you have to do?"

His voice trembled, "All of her friends are going to the funeral home tomorrow night and I've never been to a funeral home. I don't know what to say to her."

Tears came to his eyes, as I gently said, "Byron, you don't have to say one word. Just by you being there, that will mean everything to her. And if you feel you must say something, say two words—*I'm sorry.*"

"Really?" he asked. "Okay, I'm going to go to the funeral home. Thanks."

He sat for a few minutes, still not moving. I waited.

"Mom," he began softly. "I've been thinking ever since this happened that you've been traveling a lot for your job. What if something happened to you, like my friend's mom, and you died and I never got to tell you I loved you?"

His tears fell freely. Drawing a breath with a smile on my face, I said, "Thank you, my son, for telling me right now of your love. In this very moment, we have a wonderful opportunity, right now, to share our love for each other."

He stood and hugged me. This cherished moment of pure grace will stay with me for my lifetime.

MEG WAS AN eighth grader in Pennsylvania's Peters Township Middle School when I picked her up one Thursday to drive her and her friend Melissa home from after-school jazz dance class. The girls got into the car, Meg in front and Melissa in back, and buckled their seat belts.

Meg was talking loudly, clearly distressed about her day at school. "I am never going back to school—ever!"

When she took a breath I managed to interject, "Tell me, what happened?" I glanced in the rearview mirror at Melissa, huddled and frozen to the back seat.

"Well, first of all the boy I liked told everyone in the entire school he didn't like me, except he did not tell Meg Pryor! Next, my best friend since kindergarten said she wasn't my best friend anymore and maybe she wasn't ever going to be my friend. I am never going back to school!"

When Meg stopped for a breath I said, "Sometimes people say things they don't really mean. Maybe they will feel differently tomorrow."

Meg was not buying it and began yelling louder, frightening me.

At Melissa's house she thanked me hurriedly and leapt from the car. Meg began sobbing in gasps, emotion overtaking her. I turned the car into our driveway, stopped, switched the engine off, and sat silent in my seat. I reached for her, drew her to me, holding her tenderly. Tears from my sadness for her came in a steady flow as we cried together side by side. Time seemed suspended. I waited until her tears ended, both of us breathing deeply.

I heard her soft voice, "I'm okay."

"Are you sure?"

"Yes, I am sure."

We walked into the house in silence and began the evening routine of fixing and eating dinner.

The next day, back home from work, I went into the bedroom to change my clothes and saw a note propped up on my bureau. I read, "To Mom, from Meg. Thank you for yesterday. It was only when you stopped talking and you held me and cried with me that I knew how much you loved me. Love, Meg."

This lesson for my life given to me by my eight grader helps me every day to stop talking, to listen, to be in the moment with people as they tell of their sorrow.

BYRON WAS NAMED Byron David Pryor for Andy's father Byron Bell Pryor, and my father David Henry Smith. Byron was a triple legacy to Denison University in Granville, Ohio, as his grandfather Byron, Andy, and Andy's brother Ned were all graduates. The summer of 1984 before Byron's high school sophomore year, the family took a college tour to check several colleges that were possibilities for Byron. Our first stop was in Williamsburg, Virginia to see the College of William and Mary, followed by a walking tour of Williamsburg. The temperature that summer day was nearing 100 degrees with oppressive humidity. Late in the afternoon we returned to our motel to get relief from the heat and rest before refreshing ourselves for dinner.

With her pale skin Sarah was suffering from the heat. Andy and I urged her to drink water and to rest while I put cold compresses on her head. I knew it was important for her to be still, fearing she was nearing dehydration. We worried about an upset stomach so didn't give Sarah more than a snack of bread, soup, and ginger ale. There was a restaurant across the street within walking distance of the motel, so we decided to eat in shifts, giving Sarah company in the room. Meg and Byron would go to dinner without us, use Andy's credit card, tell the manager that their parents would be coming back to have dinner when the kids returned to the motel to stay with their sick sister. While Andy and I waited for them to return, Sarah rallied and asked if she could sit up and watch TV. She was our Sarah again.

When the early diners returned, Byron said, "We can take over, go enjoy your dinner. Be sure to bring something else back for Sarah to eat!"

Free to go and enjoy our dinner, we left Sarah in their hands and made our way across the roadway.

Andy and I identified ourselves to the manager when he welcomed us, chuckling, "Your son almost ate us out of the business, he ordered most everything on the menu!" (The charges on the tab reflected the appetite of a growing teen!) When we got back to the motel our three children were enjoying a show on TV, laughing just like the good times we always knew as a family.

We visited the University of Virginia the next day and headed back to Boston. Andy grew up in Newark, Ohio, with his brother Ned and his parents. With Denison University located in nearby Granville, Byron knew the campus and made an early decision to seek acceptance as a third-generation legacy.

ANDY AND BYRON loaded the car with college-bound belongings. Our son was the first to move out of state to further his education. I sat thinking again of the words from the musical, *Fiddler on the Roof*: "Sunrise, sunset. Swiftly pass the years. One season following another, laden with happiness and tears." The words reflected my life as we started out on another road trip, this time without Sarah. I would miss Byron but suspected he might be glad to be away from ongoing media coverage of Sarah's story. Perhaps it would be a relief to be where few would know the burden he bore.

One year later Meg left Boston to return to Pennsylvania as a senior at Woodland Hills High School in Pittsburgh. Meg wanted to live with Christy, her long-time friend, and Christy's parents. Reed and Carol Carpenter were delighted to care for Meg, allowing her to blossom in a new environment. Although I would miss her each day, I knew it was the right decision. Meg let us know how she was enjoying school and living with her new temporary family. She shared the good news that she auditioned for a role in the high school's senior musical, *Hello Dolly*, and was cast as Dolly.

I traveled from Boston to enjoy seeing my talented daughter perform. Surely, I was the proudest mom in the audience, especially when she received seven curtain calls. Andy couldn't get away and planned to visit at a later time to see her perform. On my return trip to Boston I pondered that Meg had made the right decision and was grateful for the Carpenters blessing my daughter with the chance to escape to a new normal.

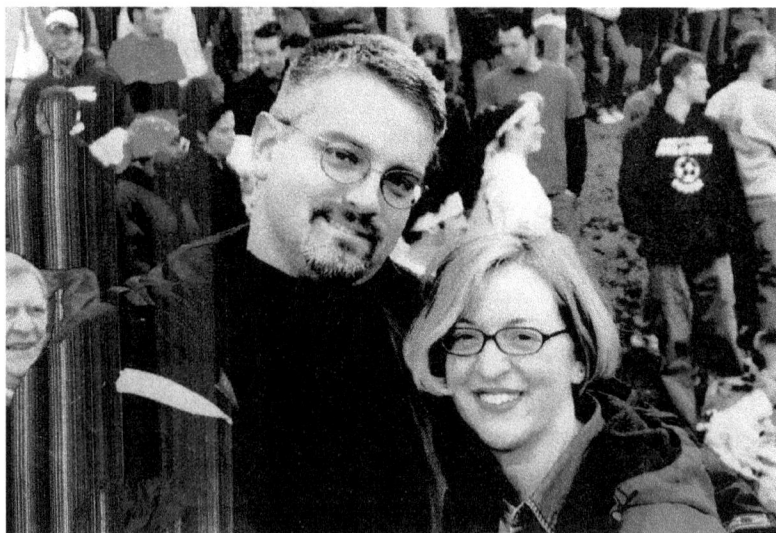

Byron and Jen at Byron's graduation from Messiah College, PA, 1991

[10] SHARING THE MESSAGE

September 1987

CHIEF OF POLICE, Cornelius J Behan of Baltimore County, Maryland, sent a note of apology to our family: "We are sorry that we could not put an end to your misery. The whole country shares your thoughts and anguish. Our thoughts and prayers are with you during this difficult time. God bless you." I felt truly blessed knowing that so many compassionate people, like Chief Behan, cared about our family. We had seen on the news that, "Police in Essex, Maryland, conduct a door-to door search for Sarah Pryor, after receiving a report that she was seen at an apartment complex there."

January 1988

THE LYRICS TO a song were playing in my head: "Help me, I am falling." I replaced "falling" with the word "failing." Help me, I am failing—trying unsuccessfully to hold my marriage together under the stress of losing Sarah. The bonds of more than twenty years of marriage had frayed and weakened under the stress of moving, constant worry about precarious finances, and Andy's frustrating and fruitless job search. Losing Sarah made everything harder as Andy self-medicated with alcohol. When Andy and I finally separated, he moved into an apartment nearby. (We separated in 1988 and would divorce in 1990.) Alone in our empty house, I wanted to find a new place to worship. I needed a small, more private space where I would not be expected to be my former out-going and cheerful self. I continued with work and counseling, trying to adjust once again to another new normal.

On Sundays I realized why my church attendance was troubling. I love children, but I felt the unfairness. With the empty Sarah space in my heart it was hard for me to be surrounded by other families. I could tolerate being with my nieces and nephews, but was emotionally exhausted by strangers' children, especially in church. Relief came when I discovered a cloister of Episcopal nuns in residence at Bethany, in the hills of Lincoln, next to Wayland, and began worshipping with them.

Thirty or so nuns had been given the mission by the Episcopal Diocese in Boston to serve mentally challenged clients. Sadly, the hundred-bed facility had been forced to give up the mission because the rural location made commuting difficult for administrative, cooking, and cleaning staff unless they could drive to work. No public transportation was available. The residents had been transferred to other facilities leaving the nuns with a spacious convent and a beautiful chapel. The Sisters of Bethany welcomed me, comforted me with their selfless love, and invited me to lunch after the service. When I drove home, I felt restored, humming the words of an old hymn, "There is a balm in Gilead, to make the wounded whole."

I worshipped with my new-found Sisters for several years until the property was sold and the order was transferred to Arlington, MA. Our last time together, Mother Superior gave me a note which read:

"Our dear, dear Barbara. You bring cheer and solace into our little family, dear friend. That is a priceless gift and all we can do is return love for love. Bless you and thank you for all you do and all you give. We keep you firmly in heart and mind and prayers; and dearest Sarah, as well. Love, Mother and Sisters."

She hugged me and gave me a brightly wrapped package. Opening it I found an old-fashioned hand-crafted wooden clown toy posed to spin on parallel bars. She said, "This toy reminds us of you, dear Barbara."

I thought, *Oh, they think I am a clown."*

She continued, "In spite of your often-upside-down world, your faith allows you to never fall off. We love you."

Their affectionate and amusing gift remains in my apartment as a reminder I can persevere even when my world seems to be turning upside down.

February 1988

BECAUSE OF SARAH'S widely publicized case as a missing child I received invitations to speak at churches, schools, and a variety of women's organizations. I adapted my talks to the audience with guidance from those who invited me by telephone or mail. My ease in speaking, encouraged by my caring heart, led me to accept engagements with the hope I could bolster others. I particularly enjoyed answering questions at the end of my talks. They gave me an idea of what people most wanted to know.

One of the letters I received after a talk came from a woman in Reading, MA:

> "Dear Barbara,
>
> "What an inspiration you were to us last evening. Your courage and faith are so outstanding, and I know we were all deeply moved. Thank you so much for coming. You will be in our thoughts and hearts.
>
> "Yours most sincerely,
>
> "Ann C., President UM Women"

Another woman heard me speak one evening at a local gathering of church women and wrote expressing her dilemma dealing with pain. She wrote:

> "I so much wanted to talk to you Monday night, but two things stopped me. One, I really didn't know how to say what was in my heart and, two, I probably would have broken down and I don't like to show that much emotion in public. It took all my self-control not to cry. Children are so innocent and beautiful. I don't understand these sick

people who do these things. It is so frightening to me."

And as was reported in *The Boston Herald*, April 24, 1988, by Joe Impemba:

Mothers share the pain of missing, murdered children

"Led by Barbara Pryor they came together to celebrate the lives of children they may never see again. Pryor, who organized the daylong event at the Sheraton Tara Hotel urged the mothers to 'put aside for an afternoon the anger and bitterness, the horror we share, to celebrate the specialness of each child.' One by one mothers, many in tears, or fighting the urge to cry, came forward to tell about their special children."

FROM AN EARLY age I have had a compassionate heart for people, especially those who are suffering. It is in my DNA I suppose. It seemed natural for me to start thinking about how I could reach out to other victims of violence I had come to know after Sarah was missing. When reading the Boston media's coverage of children who had been murdered, I felt emotionally wounded learning of the violence done to others. I remembered the cards our family received from strangers who sent greetings in care of the Wayland Police Department. It cheered me that people cared and wrote to us. I wanted to honor other victims of violence.

Springtime seemed to be the perfect time for homicide survivors to lay aside thoughts of cruelty, hate, and especially anger for one afternoon to celebrate the lives of their children. Perhaps I was the one who most needed to celebrate, remembering the joy that was mine in Sarah. On Saturday, April 23, the local Sheraton Tara Hotel sponsored the event I called Celebration of Life. My friend, Eileen Prose, of Channel Five's *Good Day* show, gave the keynote address.

Next was a time for "open microphone," an opportunity for parents to share memories of their children. I wanted us to put aside the unfairness of our losses this afternoon. The time was not meant to be for denial, but rather for a brief reprieve.

Paula Danforth talked about her namesake daughter Paula. As a toddler she stubbornly held her food in her mouth. Her daughter was murdered at age 19 while walking near her home in Sudbury, MA. Kay Dudley shared how her daughter Karen had called collect in the middle of the day when the rates were low to share some news from her life as a student at William and Mary College. Karen was killed in 1984 by a repeat offender drunk driver. Barbara Duru, mother of Frankie Barnes, described her son as liking to dance and taking tap dancing lessons. He had played a starring role as a lion in a production of Bre'r Rabbit. Frankie was murdered at the age of ten. I told about my Sarah's distorted "r" in her speech, which complicated pronunciation of her name with its three "r's". Mothers spoke when they wanted, if they wanted.

Some of the mothers urged a woman named Gert Keely to share but she was not ready. Eyeing her reluctance, I invited her to help distribute gifts of colorful butterfly soaps to each participant. As we awaited lunch, local television personality Eileen Prose gave the keynote address. After the lunch break I said there was time for anyone else who wanted to share their memories. It was then that Gert said, "I'm ready." and went to the microphone.

"Fifteen years ago my son Paul died and I became a member of Compassionate Friends, the support group for bereaved parents who've lost a child. I'm still a member. Ten years ago, I lost a second son, Joe. He was killed by a drunk driver. I became a mother of MADD (Mothers Against Drunk Driving) I'm a member still today. Five years ago, I lost a third son, Jimmy. This time my son was murdered. I became a member of Parents of Murdered Children. And that is my story." I sat speechless in amazement.

This saintly woman was doing the one thing she knew to do - to give to others. In the hush of that moment, I slowly took the microphone, tears on my cheeks.. I spoke softly, "Gert, I don't know what to say. I am overwhelmed. Your grief is my grief, only multiplied three times: "Thank you, dear lady." Although I have since lost touch with these women and the organizations they represent, as each spring arrives I think of that special day when we Celebrated Life. All of those victim Moms are part of my heart, but none has as much space as Gertrude Keely.

[11] I SAY I'M FINE, BUT . . .

SITTING IN THE car in the local market, a lengthy shopping list on my lap, I was unready for the necessary chore. I had to eat even with no appetite, but I did not move. This was a moment of escape. Alone in the car, surely no one would recognize me. I didn't want to be seen, or to talk to anybody.

What were the past week's events that had catapulted me into this emotional challenge? I was in the midst of a job search. A re-organization and staff downsizing had ended my work at Bradford School. Andy was still not employed, and he trustingly had talked with a *Boston Herald* news reporter about our financial troubles. She was motivated to publish our challenges in hopes of stimulating someone to hire one of us. The revelation of our financial woes to the greater Boston area left me feeling exposed and vulnerable. I wanted to hide but I had to buy groceries. Reluctantly I opened the car door and prayed for courage as I walked across the crowded parking lot. Suddenly someone called my name. Turning around I met an acquaintance who greeted me with a smile and a question.

"How are you?"

I returned her smile on automatic response, "I'm fine, thank you."

Mary looked at me with kind eyes, seeing me as my wounded self. Tenderly she said, "Really?"

I heard myself respond, "No, really, I am not fine." Heaving sobs came from deep inside me. I felt Mary pull me into her loving arms. She held me for some minutes as I sobbed into her shoulder. We stood in that parking lot as I allowed myself to be comforted and loved for a moment by this caring angel mom.

At home, unloading groceries, still reeling from the exposure, I answered the phone to hear people ask if I could drive a sit-down lawn mower, or do a myriad of tasks, readers of the paper offering ideas about possible jobs. Then the call came that changed my life. The CEO of T.J. Maxx, Ben Cammarata, had read the article and asked his administrative assistant, Rhonda, to call to request my resume. Promptly I delivered it to Rhonda and was shocked by the turn of events that followed. The next day she phoned to say Ben wanted me to have two informational interviews, one in their Hit or Miss home office, and one with the human resources department at T.J. Maxx's home office. Andy and I had met Ben several months before when we had been investigating the possibility of establishing a non-profit organization on behalf of missing children.

Within three days I had visited Hit or Miss and then the Framingham home office of T.J. Maxx. Marg Balcom, head of TJM's recruitment, talked with me while looking over job openings and reviewing my experience and skills. She had developed an in-house career development program which she thought would be a good fit with my abilities, but the current employee in the position was hoping to find a way to be a stay-at-home mom with her new baby. I left Marg's office at 5:00 p.m. with her promise to keep in touch.

The next day her secretary called to say that just after I left, the current program director gave her resignation notice, having solved her child care problem by caring for an additional child in her home. Marg asked if I could begin work at T.J. Maxx on Monday morning. This was the beginning of the best career of my life. I am indebted to Ben and Marg.

April 1988

FROM APRIL 1988, for eleven rewarding years the T.J. Maxx Human Resources Department in the home office was a perfect fit for my abilities and experience. I loved the work I did and I cherished the co-workers and friends I met during the time I worked for the company. Here's the CEO's memo welcoming me.

To: Barbara Pryor

From: Ben Cammarata

Date: April 27, 1988

Congratulations! I knew that T.J. Maxx and Barbara Pryor were meant for each other! I wish you a long and successful career with our company.

May 1988

WITH DIRECTIONS IN hand, I left my home one evening to drive to a church on the north shore of Boston. A gaggle of friendly members welcomed me and ushered me into the church's sanctuary. I had thought I would speak in the informality of the church hall, not from the pastor's pulpit. A member of the planning committee attached a microphone to my lapel as I moved closer to the audience. *Everything will be fine*, I assured myself as the church began filling with a large audience. Looking around the hall I saw I faced a new challenge. What were children doing in my audience? I had thought the evening was for adults. I had some difficult material to discuss, information which was not child-friendly. Worse yet, three of the children were girls, all about Sarah's age with blonde hair like Sarah's. I would have to think quickly, scan through my talk, delete some material, but still have it make sense. I prayed, *Help me get over this stress.*

Taking a deep breath, putting on a smile, I felt some peace as I began my talk. The three Sarah look-alikes sat together with their eyes focused on me. The talk finished to applause, and I was shown into the Fellowship Hall where refreshments and members of the audience greeted me. When I spotted the three little ladies, the perkiest of the trio asked if she could give me a hug, "since Sarah wasn't around anymore." Her embrace was an unexpected warm and wonderful gift. My changed attitude about children in the audience gave me a surprise and an unforgettable blessing.

ONE OF THE distractions in the silent days without the company of Sarah, was serving on The Women's Hospitality and Fellowship Committee at Wayland's Trinitarian Church. The members organized a Mother's Day brunch dedicated to mothers, grandmothers, and daughters. The sun was shining in azure skies with white puffy clouds this Saturday in May. In the festive room, I admired tables with centerpieces of yellow and white daises and pink carnations. Food scents filled the air, the aroma of freshly baked bread mixed with a hint of bacon to be offered as a side dish. I was in my favorite role as greeter and welcomed the guests, helping them find seats. Others began delivering plates with omelets, fruit, breads, and pastries. Conversations hummed at the tables as a pianist played a medley of tunes. Seeing the celebration was running smoothly I settled in my chair to enjoy the event and music in honor of mothers. For a moment I thought of Meg at college and my mother unable to come to the celebration, and of my longing for Sarah.

A soloist began singing and suddenly I felt a sharp pang of dread so powerful that I struggled to breathe. My mind filled with panic as I thought, *What am I doing here? All these mothers have their daughters, except for me. I want to get up and leave before my tears ruin everything.* Instead of fleeing I began to tell myself, *Act your way through this moment—do it for them.* Regaining my composure, I held it together through the meal and the entertainment and worked with my church friends to clean up the kitchen. I drove home physically exhausted and emotionally spent, relieved I no longer had to put a pretend smile on my face.

The next week I received a hand-written note from a teenager I did not know who had attended the brunch with her neighbor, my friend Jane. I read, "Once I was seated at my table at the Mother's Day brunch, I recognized you as Sarah Pryor's mother. I took courage from you, knowing how difficult it must be for you. I want to thank you because you don't know how much you helped me."

Reading further I was shocked to learn that her mother had committed suicide the year before. This precious 17-year-old, a junior at Wayland High School, had come home from school to find her mother on the floor. I sat for long moments trying to absorb the enormity of the message, then rereading the note. While processing the grief of this young girl's unimaginable tragedy I cried for both our losses. Lifting a prayer of thanksgiving, I wrote to tell her of my gratitude for her brave and generous encouragement.

July 16, 1988

"Search resumes in Pryor case. Sand pit excavated after reported tip from inmate. Investigators began digging at a sand pit in the central Massachusetts town of Berlin. State Police, using a 15-ton bulldozer and a dog trained to find the scent of cadavers as they combed the 22-acre sand pit, located in a remote area near the Wachusett Reservoir. According to a source familiar with the search, investigators received a tip from an inmate in a state prison that Pryor's body had been buried at the pit."

—*Boston Globe*, July 16, 1988, Peter J. Howe

EARLY AFTERNOON ON a hectic Thursday at my job at TJ Maxx it seemed to me that many of the home office employees had not made the connection that I was the mother of missing Sarah Pryor. Every working day I struggled to leave the weight of my grief in the parking lot, and to separate my personal agony from my professional life, but this day became a challenge. Tom Reilly, the District Attorney, called saying, "I hate to bother you at work, but you've asked that we let you know when something is about to break in the media. Based on a lead from an inmate in prison we were searching a sandpit in Berlin, Massachusetts, and the media arrived in droves. (Berlin is about 18 miles from Wayland.) The crowd of reporters has distracted the body dogs and we've had to call off the search until tomorrow, but the media will have it on the news tonight. We believe that the lead will turn out to be false, but now the media has it. I'm sorry."

I ended the conversation with my thanks, then sat for a still and empty moment, before moving into action to warn the family. Sitting in front of the television news that evening with them, I watched the latest in Sarah Pryor news coverage that was always hard to absorb, as it was raw and hurtful.

The next morning at work I secluded myself in my office, asking that my phone calls be diverted. I especially did not want to talk to the media. Working easily in solitude, feeling safe in my isolation, concentrating, losing track of time, I heard a soft knock on the door.

"Come in," I said. The door opened, and there were nine co-workers with a spokesperson holding a large vase of sunny yellow rose buds.

"These are from all of us. We want you to know that we are thinking of you and that we love you."

As I accepted the vase I saw the flowers more clearly. Each rose had a yellow ribbon tied to it with a Thinking of You card signed by a co-worker. Overwhelmed by the love filling the room, I managed a thank you through my tears. The cards said things like:

"Keeping you in mind at this time,"

"You are a wonderful person and a good friend,"

"You are a strong and wonderful lady,"

"You are a good friend and a beautiful person,"

"I wish I can be more like you,"

"I love you and I care,"

and "You and Sarah are in all our prayers."

Saturday's *Boston Globe* and *Boston Herald* relayed the same news: "The twenty-two-acre excavation and the search for Sarah's body in the Berlin Massachusetts sandpit is finished. The Middlesex District Attorney Tom Reilly is quoted, 'The cruel hoax is over.'"

Tom's comment, "The cruel hoax is over" made me think, *It is not over, it just keeps going on unendingly. I cannot stop the roller coaster ride. There is no way to end the cruelty of those who lie; who do not care what hurt they inflict.* Drearily reflecting on another unsuccessful body search, the memory of the yellow roses brought me a smile. Long after those flowers died, I will have the memory of those messages of comfort knowing how much I am loved by those who work with me and matter to me.

The weekend after the media reported the lie about Sarah's remains being buried in the Berlin gravel pit, I was scheduled to attend my church's annual women's retreat of prayer, fasting, and silent contemplation at a retreat center an hour away from Wayland. I welcomed the weekend eager to be out of the public eye and because I knew Christopher Leighton, the young pastor leading the spiritual part of the retreat.

He gave a talk on Friday evening then instructed us to honor silence until the breakfast meal. The quiet was welcome because I was in fresh pain, feeling betrayed by two unknown young men incarcerated for murder who told the gravel pit lies about Sarah. I longed to feel some peace of mind. Silence and the darkness brought the two enemies of my faith—fear and doubt, which now so crowded my thinking—that my sleep was troubled. I welcomed the morning, the lifting of silence, the food at breakfast. We moved to another room to hear speakers who provided renewed hope through their inspirational talks

Christopher ended the morning telling us that after lunch we would have a long afternoon break to rest, relax, and enjoy the gardens on the grounds of the center. He would be available for personal talks in our free time if we wished. I finished my lunch and hurried to his door eager to meet with him, but unable to keep from crying as he welcomed me into the room.

Before he could speak, I blurted, "Help me. I'm trying to forgive Sarah's killer and I cannot do it."

Taking my hand gently in his, speaking in a quiet voice he said, "My precious child, you don't have to forgive, nor can you do it on your own. It is too big for anyone! God is the only one who can do it in place of us. Do you want me to ask Him to help you to forgive?"

I nodded a yes. He prayed for the gift of forgiveness, to hate the evil, but not the one who did evil. There was no instant earth-shaking change in me, but my mind did become quiet, peaceful, like a black board washed clean. The prayer had wiped away anxiety, cleared my mind of inner noise, and calmed my thoughts with a new peace, as I received the gift of forgiveness meant for me, not the doer of evil.

There was room now to fill my heart with the joyful spirit of my Sarah.

[12] A LIGHT
BREAKS THROUGH

THE LATE AUTHOR, *Corrie ten Boom* became my spiritual hero after I read the World War II memoir of her Dutch family's secret hiding place—the closet-like rooms where Jews were harbored until they could be moved away from the Germans who had invaded Holland.

Corrie was the sole family survivor of the German concentration camps. Once released from her captivity at age fifty, she gave lectures around the world about God's forgiveness until she was into her nineties. She quoted her sister's frequent saying, "There is no pit so deep that God is not deeper still." Corrie wrote a letter in June 1945, to Jan Vogel, the Dutch collaborator who had betrayed her family's hiding place to the Nazis. She wrote:

"I heard today that you are very probably the person who betrayed me. I went through ten months in concentration camp. My father died in prison after ten days and my sister after ten months. I have forgiven you everything. God will forgive you, too, if you ask Him. He loves you and sent His son to pay the price for your sins, to bear the punishment for you and me. You need to give an answer to that. When He says, "Come to me, give me your heart," then your answer must be, 'Yes, Lord, Make me your child.'"

Jan Vogel was caught, arrested, brought to trial, and sentenced to death. Reading the book I was uplifted by her outpouring of forgiveness. I remembered how Sarah had also taught a lesson in forgiveness. Several weeks after Sarah was missing I found a paper she had completed in her Sunday School class. There were three questions the children were to answer:

1. How do people know you are a Christian? Sarah: "We have a Bible in our house and we have a manger scene at Christmas time."

2. Do you share with people that you are a Christian? Sarah: "No, I'm shy!"

3. By watching how you act, how do people know that you are a Christian? Sarah: "I forgive them."

At nine years old Sarah knew the importance of forgiveness. If she could, then her mom could. I gave the gift of forgiveness to myself to lift the burden of grief and return love to my heart. I would honor the blessed spirit of the child I had for a short time. Her spirit will never die. I hope that people who come into my life can see Sarah shining through me. I changed how I live my life because of how Sarah lived hers.

August 8, 1988

The Commonwealth Of Massachusetts

Executive Office of Human Services

Parole Board

100 Cambridge Street, Boston 02202

August 8 , 1988

Dear Mr. and Mrs. Pryor,

This is to advise you that the Massachusetts Parole Board has decided to release Laura Cancel Hawkins from custody. This release is now scheduled to take place on 8/26/88. He/She will be under the supervision of (a) Parole Officer (Region 1) while on parole.

Yours truly,

Marian F. Young

Parole Officer

Boston State Pre-Release

I OPENED THIS letter from the Massachusetts Parole Board and read that Laura Hawkins, that boastful perjurer, had been released from prison. I had thought that justice would prevail and she would spend much more time incarcerated for her horrible lies. What a big letdown for me.

The pain came again, raw and raging, bursting suddenly with a burning I felt in my body and soul. With the recent letter from the Parole Board and continual coverage by the news media of suspected sightings of Sarah or the dreaded message of a search for a body, I seemed constantly on high alert. I often said, "Fine," to the question, "How are you?" with the automatic response of a tightly programmed robot. I worked each day, though my soul seemed far away.

One day a co-worker interrupted my thoughts with a message that something had been delivered for me in the lobby of our large office building. I walked down three flights of stairs without noticing anyone who passed, my mind preoccupied with a myriad of thoughts. At the reception area, I asked for my package. The receptionist handed me another bouquet of yellow roses in a brightly wrapped vase with a card attached, "You are a beacon of light for us. We see and feel your pain. Love, Your work-friends."

Suddenly a light broke through my emotional darkness and my soul was reconnected. A second gift of flowers the color of the sun; the color of Sarah's beautiful blonde hair; and the color to remember lost or missing soldiers. I thought of a morning I had looked out our family room window and discovered the tree in our front yard had been adorned with dozens of yellow ribbons during the night. Holding the vase of yellow roses from my co-workers I returned to my office with a smile on my face eager to thank my colleagues for another thoughtful and generous love gift from them.

ONE OF THE hardest questions the parent of a missing or dead child has to answer is, "How many children do you have?" I suppose I answer differently depending on how I know the person or if I sense their sympathy. If I answer that I have three children, I am not being truthful. Sarah is no longer with us. If however, I answer that I have just two children, I feel that I am neglecting Sarah, wiping her memory away. I decided the right answer for me was saying, "I have two living children, a son and a daughter, and I have a little girl who is in heaven."

The person who asks the question can invite me to explain further or be satisfied with my statement. Byron and Meg have also experienced the paradox of wanting their sister's story to be private yet feeling that their silence dishonors Sarah's memory. In the long years of waiting without answers, I sometimes struggled with what I said was "worrying" but truth be told it was really "fear." I wrote this poem in hopes that I would honestly face my feelings and gain the courage to put an end to any moment of fear:

THE LONG-DISTANCE RUNNER (AKA FEAR)

Fear is an agile, strong and powerful athlete.

He races relentlessly in raw competition.

In contrast, Faith seems to be a short distance runner,

accomplishing bursts of victory.

Formidable Fear seems to outwit and out last his
opponent Faith.

He is single-minded. His objective is to win at all costs.

He takes off in a split second from the starting block,

pulling ahead of Faith and me.

111

He entices me to catch up to his majestic lead.

As he outdistances me, I notice he becomes larger in stature.

He seems overpowering and I lose speed. -slowing down.

I stumble, I give in. I fall.

What will I do?

Give up?

Or... Get up and keep running to victory?

September 1988

THE OPPORTUNITY CAME to be a volunteer supporting Scott Harshbarger in his bid to be the next governor of Massachusetts. Scott had been District Attorney of Middlesex County in 1985 when Sarah was missing. I appreciated his professionalism and concern for our family in our meetings with him. Bob, a fellow campaign worker, offered me a ticket to the party's fundraiser—dinner at one of Boston's downtown hotels. The keynote speaker for the gala affair was Missouri's Representative Richard Gephardt, then minority whip in Congress, whom I had known in college at Northwestern University where he served as Student Senate President and I was one of two Senior Senators

That evening I was excited to see Rich and was properly attired in a black cocktail dress as I entered the ballroom. Loud laughter, music, and chatter filled the packed room as people mingled. Looking closely, I saw politicians near me including Senator Ted Kennedy and Governor Mike Dukakis. Then Rich Gephardt came into the room and I reached out to touch his shoulder as he made his way through the crowd. He recognized me, and we hugged as friends seeing each other many years later. We chatted briefly before he excused himself to go to the head table. I took my place at one of the tables. The noise and activity surrounding me made me feel like a child at a three-ring-circus.

I focused on place settings for each diner that seemed to go on endlessly with forks and spoons. The food arrived in multiple courses: appetizers, soups, salads, sherbet to clear your palate, and entrees looking as if they should be photographed for a gourmet magazine. I tried to pick up the correct eating utensil, slyly following the lead of others at my table as they enjoyed talking with each other while they ate. Because I was so focused on the tableware and the food set before me I had not noticed the wait staff delivering the many courses. The servers were faceless to me as I concentrated on the dinner and assembled dignitaries.

When it was time for the main course the waitress placed a plate in front of me. Reading my name tag and leaning forward she whispered, "Barbara Pryor? Sarah Pryor's mother?"

Now looking directly at the woman speaking to me I smiled and replied, "Yes, I am Sarah Pryor's mother."

She leaned close to my ear, "I have prayed for Sarah and your family every day since she was taken."

The world seemed to stop spinning for a second as I took in the enormity of her devotion. Making sure to take a breath I said, "Thank you. Your prayers have helped me. Thank you again."

That night walking into my apartment I understood that I was at the fundraiser simply to receive the kind message of a woman I had at first not even noticed. She and countless others have been the wind beneath my wings. I am humbled and deeply grateful.

PART THREE:
SARAH'S LEGACY

[13] News &

Memories

"Sometimes when one person is missing, the whole world seems de-populated."

—A. De Lamartine

Late 1988

CHRISTOPHER DARDEN, lead prosecutor in the O.J. Simpson trial, was in Boston as a speaker at the annual Crime Victims' Conference. I went to meet him and to share our experience as victims of a violent crime. Christopher told me that his mother's only sister was murdered. In addition to that loss, his best friend's 17-year-old son was shot to death because he refused to give up his Sony Walkman. Darden said, "I am appalled at the carnage and the destruction that is done by the media, without regard to the suffering of the victim families. I don't think you can walk in, get your story, and walk out leaving the crime victims to be 'yesterday's news.' You can't just take; you have to give back, become part of the responsibility and fulfill your obligation. You aren't around a year later, you don't call a year later on the anniversary of a loved one's death and say, 'I want you to know I'm thinking of you today.' That's not the way it happens. What's real for the media is often, 'I needed you and your story a year ago. You are not needed anymore.' "

Darden's words ring true for many victims. I was grateful he shared his experience and wisdom with me. I care about crime victims who are subjected to heedless harassment.

April 1989

A LETTER CAME from Richard Nelson Bolles, author of *What Color is Your Parachute*, and *Three Boxes of Life and How to Get Out of Them*:

> "Dear Barbara,
>
> "I was grateful to receive your touching letter, I appreciated all your warm and kind words about my books, and particularly The Epilogue in *Three Boxes*. I was deeply touched to read your words in the loss of your own nine-year-old. My wife and I have a darling thirteen-year-old girl, and if anything happened to her, I would be devastated. I shall use your quote.

"My faith has meant so much to me, as I guess yours has to you, that I marvel at anyone who tries to live without it. Your letter meant a great deal to me. I thank you ever so much, Barbara, for taking the time and trouble to write it. Godspeed, and God bless you.

"Faithfully,

"Dick Bolles"

August 1989

THE CAR WAS packed again, this time with Meg's belongings as we drove west to the University of Massachusetts in Amherst, MA. She chatted endlessly about starting her freshmen year in college. I had assured myself that having her leave high school and home would not be a big adjustment for me. She would be living a mere three hours away from my Framingham apartment. I had not considered that she was the second daughter who would be leaving—first Sarah, now Meg. I phoned my mother at her assisted living facility, promising I would take her to dinner when I returned from settling Meg into her dorm room.

On campus we became part of a long parade of cars bearing enthusiastic students and their parents. After computers, a microwave, a small refrigerator, and lamps were sandwiched in among dressers, desks, and beds in Meg's room she and I hugged and parted. I rejoined the parade of emptier cars, driven by parents leaving their children. At the first toll booth at the entrance to the Massachusetts Turnpike the enormity of what was happening hit me. My Meg was starting a new chapter in her life, college, and that would make everything different for us. I felt the blow of losing a daughter again. I pulled into a rest area realizing I needed to cancel dinner plans with my mother because I was emotionally exhausted. I blew my nose, mustered a pleasant telephone voice, and asked her for a rain-check. At home I fell into bed wishing for sleep to end my troubling day.

The next morning was not better for I had to deal again with opening day for local schools after summer vacation. The yellow school buses reminded me that another year had sped by without Sarah. My head throbbed, I decided I would not go to work. With temporary composure, I phoned an excuse, then dropped to the living floor weeping uncontrollably. Through my sobs I heard a rapping at my door and the voice of our building's young maintenance man.

"Barbara, I saw your parked car, I was worried about you." With red, swollen eyes I opened the door to greet an angel, this one in the uniform of a caring building custodian.

January 13, 1990
Sarah's 14th Birthday

Marking the Years with Thoughts of Happier Times

"One of the things that got lost in Boston (during the Charles Stuart crime coverage) was January 13th, which was the 14th birthday of a little girl who was kidnapped in October 1985. Sarah Pryor is long presumed dead, and in Boston she is forgotten. Her mother did not forget the date, as she will not forget her daughter. Barbara Pryor wrote an open letter to her Sarah on her birthday."

—*Boston Herald,* January 21, 1990, by Norma Nathan

Here is my letter to Sarah:

"This would be your 14th birthday. Wasn't it just last year I held you in my arms in the still quiet of the hospital, marveling at your precious parts? You were tiny compared to your hefty brother and sister and your ears were just a bit big. But I loved you, and we were bonded forever.

"Wasn't it only last month, you persistently pleaded; "Please, can I have nine friends for a sleepover on my ninth birthday? We'll sleep and do everything you say!" Although I was recovering from back surgery, I had agreed. Your friends assembled at the party. I lasted until after you opened your birthday gifts, then— sleepily I retired to bed leaving your Dad and Meg in charge.

"At 2:30 in the morning, I was awakened by gleeful laughter from downstairs. I gingerly descended the staircase to see what was going on in the middle of the night. When I reached your circle of friends, I said in my motherly-stern voice, "What are you doing?" Then I noticed ten heads soapy wet with shampoo.

"We're playing beauty-parlor," you announced!

"I'm sure it was only last week that you sobbed—you didn't want to leave your three friends and move far away to Boston. Why did you weep uncontrollably? Did you feel the shortness of your own little life? It seems only yesterday, that you walked in innocent joy on that beautiful fall day— excited to be taking a walk on a warm sunshiny afternoon. I thought I would sing Happy Birthday, but today it feels as if the lonely sadness will never leave me."

Late January 1990

AMONG THE INVESTIGATORS who worked tirelessly on Sarah's case were John McEvoy, Tom Reilly, Joe Flaherty, Peter Sennett, Joe Moynihan, and Kevin O'Shea. After a particularly grotesque and well-publicized crime, the Charles Stuart case, I focused on the steadfast work the investigators did in their daily commitment to their jobs. It helped me to move beyond the ugliness of a brutal crime. I thought of the criminal justice professionals who worked tirelessly on Sarah's case, those who were dedicated, and deeply committed to the communities they served.

I asked John McEvoy, a prosecuting attorney in the Middlesex County District Attorney's office, "Why do you stay in this ugly business every day? What keeps you doing what you do day after day when you deal with people who do bad things to innocent people? You could be making money in a prestigious law firm!"

John laughed. "I haven't thought about that for a long time." He paused, then said, "If I can't make a difference for the victim, which often I can't, I hope I make a difference for the victim's family."

When the media exposes another violent crime, I have a burning sense of betrayal and heartache, but I remind myself of public servants like John and I say to the evil-doers in the world, "You have not won!"

February 8, 1990

Witness, Violent Past Tie Man to Pryor Case

"A convicted murderer, who served time for trying to abduct a Newton woman (11/9/1985) was standing near the spot where Sarah Pryor was last seen on October 9, 1985, a witness has told Middlesex County Authorities probing the girl's disappearance. While the witness account and the suspect's history of violence against women has made him a suspect in Pryor's (case) sources close to the case say there is no physical evidence against him . . . For the Newton attack the suspect was sentenced to 4-7 years for kidnapping, and to a concurrent term of 3-5 years for assault with a dangerous weapon. Last year, as he neared the end of his sentences at Norfolk State Prison, District Attorney Thomas Reilly obtained a court order preventing his release until

Dallas (Texas) authorities could apply for the suspect's return."

—*The Boston Globe*, February 8, 1990

Kevin Cullen and Ray Richard

[14] PROFESSIONAL HELP

June 1990

JOE MOYNIHAN WAS one of the brightest and best officers working on Sarah's case. In his early 30s, he was a dashingly handsome bachelor. Joe, assigned to the Middlesex District Attorney's office, dealt each day with the creeps of the world. He worked the drug detail, child pornography, and other gruesome cases. He knew evil— he saw it every day, criminals with no moral compass. Joe helped me gain a new perspective that drastically changed my thoughts about Sarah and her whereabouts. Joe was driving me to a meeting at the DA's office.

"Barbara, if Sarah were alive, she would be living a life far worse than death. I believe she would be unrecoverable."

I sat shocked into silence by what he said, but his statement moved me to begin adjusting my dreams of rescue and recovery. Sarah was not living happily with a grandmother and grandfather in a cozy cottage somewhere. Sarah was either dead or she was living a life of dread. I decided to think of Sarah happily living with God, safely in his loving arms.

In June of 1990 Joe Moynihan departed with an FBI agent from Boston in a small plane headed for Maine and FBI training. Joe and the agent crashed in fog over Greenville, Maine. Both died on impact. I learned that when Joe's wallet was recovered Sarah's picture was found tucked in a pocket. I said a silent, *Thank you, Joe. Sarah was never far from your thoughts and your heart.* I wrote this poem for his mom and his sister. I wrote this poem for me.

To Joe,

Your death, so shocking and
wretched, sheds a dark shadow on our
souls. May the forever of you and love
bear the darkness of this hour away from
our hearts.

WELCOME TO OUR PLACE

So now you've gone and we are left with
sorrow

so deep and so wide that we feel we will
drown.

The sadness is of epidemic proportions,
　　so intrusive that we

dare not speak too much or for too long
　　for fear we'll pull each other under

into the sea of hopelessness and doom.

Your words of both shock and clarity
　　come crashing into my mind—again

and again.

That day you had driven me to Cambridge
　　for a briefing at the Middlesex District
　　　　Attorney's office

you had moved from casual conversation
　　into blunt and frightening honesty.

I was caught in the web of unreal hope,
born from my desire to have my story end
　　　　my way

happily ever after.

I was ensnared in the trap of wishing

and wanting;

pushing from my naïve and frightened
　　　　mind

the reality of evil that you knew and faced

in the daily doing of your job.

"Barbara," you had said with a directness
　　and clarity that stopped me short.

"Barbara," you had continued . . .

"There are worse things than death.

If Sarah were alive,

she would most likely be forced

to live a life far worse than death.

Believe me on this one. Trust me."

How brave of you to share what I most
needed to hear.

No matter the pain in my heart

no matter the silly dreams and

rescue scenes that had been deluding my
mind.

How courageous of you.

And I am reminded of your courage that
day

years ago

and of the shift that began to occur in my
thinking

and today, I thank you.

Even if death has taken you early

it warms me to think of

the welcome you are receiving on that
side.

You have found our girls . . .

Sarah and Cathy.

Sarah, the forever bouncing and excited
greeter,

and Cathy, somewhat more reserved,
playing it cool,

but nonetheless, both of them

welcoming you with open arms,

Saying, "Hey, Joe, Welcome to our Place."

September 1990

"Grief is a curious thing when it happens unexpectedly. It is a Band-Aid being ripped away, taking the top layer off a family."

—Jodi Picoult, *My Sister's Keeper*

AFTER JOE'S FUNERAL I drove to my empty home and felt completely alone. Byron was at Messiah College near Gettysburg, PA, while Meg was attending the University of Massachusetts at Amherst. Joe's death brought back vividly the loss of Sarah but added to it I was grieving the loss of my marriage. Andy and I had recently signed divorce papers. We had tried to deal together with our grief, we had attended Compassionate Friends, a group for parents who have experienced the death of a child. We had steadfast support from our church, our community, the criminal justice system, and we had our faith, yet our marriage failed. Emotionally exhausted, I began weeping in the silence of the living room on Concord Road. *What is wrong with me? I've always been able to cope. I've toughed it through so many situations. What happened that I could no longer deal in my marriage?*

I decided to get professional help to sort out these questions. I hoped to find a caring and competent person to listen as I attempted to clear the ongoing conversations in my head, many of which I was sure were self-centered and unhelpful. The counselor told me that statistics of marriages staying together in Andy and my circumstances were extremely low. We had lost our child which altered each of our lives traumatically. Secondly, when death is sudden the burden is greater for each parent to bear. Finally, someone had done unimaginable evil to one we both loved.

In addition to suffering about Sarah I mourned the loss of my marriage and began to face the responsibility I had in its failure. Andy and I agreed to sell our Wayland house and new owners soon occupied the house we had lived in since 1985. I rented an apartment in nearby Framingham settling near my workplace. Then I began thinking of ways to volunteer for some worthy cause in an effort to occupy not only the empty hours, but to bring gladness to my heart. I rekindled a way to serve that helped me fill the spare time on my hands.

After attending the Women's Cursillo weekend in 1980 I accepted leadership roles in the Pittsburgh area over the next five years. When I served on a team with other lay leaders and clergy I always came home renewed in spirit. When we came to New England in 1985, Andy and I continued to serve in leadership roles in the Boston Cursillo communities—Andy on the Men's Episcopal team while I answered the call to serve with my Roman Catholic sisters. Meeting new friends and serving on various teams allowed me to temporarily put aside my chaotic thoughts during long days of waiting for answers about Sarah.

An opportunity came to serve as leader in a weekend retreat for one hundred women incarcerated at the nearby Massachusetts Correctional Institute in Framingham (MCI). I welcomed the chance to meet the women and encourage them to maintain a hopeful spirit. The women welcomed me warmly, having seen me as Sarah's mom on TV. The weekend of the retreat sped by and I left the grounds with renewed hope for their lives in spite of the walls of the prison. Their Sunday evenings were set aside for celebrating the mass and I accepted an invitation to join them in worship. The chaplain, a woman of strong faith, took me under her wing. Recognizing my gifts of encouragement coupled with my experience in career counseling, she asked if I would coach several women ready to be released.

The Prison Chaplain made arrangements for me to meet one-to-one with four women each week. Each woman and I worked together to prepare her to re-enter a world which would present tough challenges. The focus of my coaching was to help the women think their way through possible complications. We talked about steps they could take to avoid returning to prison. I was aware that many of the incarcerated women had taken on guilt that was not theirs, but rather belonged to the men in their lives. We talked about building healthy communities of support, so they could be protected from the destructive patterns that had brought trouble into their lives.

March 1992

IN ADDITION TO continuing with one-to-one counseling, I joined a small group of women who were working to heal emotional wounds from childhood. Two mental health professionals led our weekly meetings. At one evening meeting, I was surprised to recover my own frightening childhood memory which I shared. I was six-years-old, living in the small town of Washington, Pennsylvania. I walked to and from Sixth Ward School with several children from the neighborhood. We walked in the morning to school, came home at lunchtime, and returned to school for the rest of the school day.

My best friend Lois lived across the street. I noticed one day that my mother had changed the rules for visiting her. Instead of crossing the street by myself, my mother now insisted that she come onto the porch to watch me cross the short distance to my friend's house. In addition,

I noticed that my mother began repeatedly to warn me against talking to strangers. I sensed something had happened but she did not tell me why she treated me so differently. Years later I learned a young girl in the Pittsburgh area had let someone into her house when her mother took a short trip to the grocery store. The girl had been murdered.

One day, late leaving my first-grade classroom, I had to walk home alone. The sixth-grade crossing guard held a stop sign allowing me to cross the street safely and I turned down the familiar sidewalk to my house. I noticed a car was parked at the curb with a man in the driver's seat. He rolled down the car window and began talking to me but I couldn't hear what he was saying. As I moved closer to his car he quickly opened the passenger door.

When he leaned toward me I screamed a blood-curdling scream and ran away as fast as I could down a steep hill, never stopping for at least six city blocks until I reached a friend's house at the bottom of my street. Judy's mother alerted mine and Mom came to get me. I thought I was in trouble because I had talked to a stranger. Mother calmly fed me lunch and drove me back to school in spite of my protests that I was scared.

Back in the classroom I became absorbed in first grade activities and forgot the terrifying moments I had experienced until a secretary came to bring me to the principal's office. I thought, *I must really be in trouble.* At the office the secretary opened the door and I stood frozen. There stood the principal, my mother, my father, two very tall State Police Officers and the man that had been sitting in the car. I was afraid and confused.

What I remembered in my adult years of that scary moment was the principal explaining the man had only been asking me directions to my school. He was a salesman for school supplies and he was lost. I was filled with shame, embarrassed that I caused the man to be in trouble. I would never forget what my mother said to me as we left the room that day. "I would have been scared to death of that man. He has the bushiest eyebrows I have ever seen."

Now, in 1990 when I sat in my women's group and recounted my experience as a six-year-old, I felt my lungs hurt with the same intensity I had felt that day running down the hill to escape. The mental health professionals helped me to realize my screams were not based on fear that I had disobeyed my parents by getting close to a stranger. The primal screams clearly meant I had been in imminent danger. The man had lunged for me. He was trying to take me using the child predator technique of asking for directions. He had an evil intention about a young child, but that day he got away with it. I was not mistaken. What I did that day by running away from the situation likely saved my life. How I regretted that I had never warned my children.

One day on a drive with my mother I asked her if she remembered that time in first grade when we were in the principal's office. She echoed the exact words she had said to me forty-five years earlier, "I remember that man and he had the bushiest eyebrows I had ever seen."

[15] A Caring Touch

October 26, 1993

I WROTE "Honoring Holly" as a tribute to Holly Piirainen and gave the poem to her family at her funeral in western Massachusetts. Ten-year-old Holly was visiting her grandmother and walked over to a neighbor's house to see their new puppy. Her murdered body was recovered days later, but the crime has not been solved.

HONORING HOLLY

Precious daughter, Lively sister, Beloved
grandchild, Charming niece, Delightful

classmate, Fun friend, and Cheerful neighbor.

—Taken from those who cared for her and about her

~

Taken . . . stolen, with malice, with intent and with greed.

Without regard, without caring.

Consumed, then discarded, thrown away, disposed, trashed.

Not caring, senseless, Insane and inhumane.

Gone. Gone the laughter. Gone the smiles, the hugs, the kisses, and the chatter.

Silenced, the earthly being, her right to be, her capacity to become. Silenced.

Taken.

We are left here and now. Whatever shall we do? How can we go on?

We care so much, and evil does not care at all.

Evil doer of this deed, this murderer, this robber of the precious, priceless.

Holly Piirainen, jewel that was ours.

Rest in peace, in joy and in love.

March 1994

AN INVITATION CAME to be a guest on the Geraldo Rivera television show for a program called, Psychic Detectives, featuring the parents of three missing children and three psychics and the crimes they said they had helped solve. That day I arrived at New York's JFK Airport and met Ben Ermini, the Director of the National Center for Missing and Exploited Children, to share a cab to the studio where we were shown into the green room. There I met two other mothers who were traveling my lost child journey: Noreen Gosch of West Des Moines, Iowa, the mother of 12-year-old Johnny who had been kidnapped while delivering newspapers in September, 1982, and Rosemary Glover whose two-year-old son Shaun had been snatched from a Manhattan playground as Rosemary watched. Eighteen months had passed since she had seen her baby.

I heard each mother's story, realizing that although our circumstances were different, we all felt each other's pain. The makeup call interrupted my thoughts as Greta Alexander and John Gatchings, psychics, introduced themselves. They explained that the third psychic had found herself lost on the way to the studio. (I silently chuckled at the thought of that absurdity.)

Without any knowledge of Sarah's specific case to bias their view they both told me they believed that Sarah was murdered. I heard what they said without showing emotion because this was what Sarah's investigative team also believed. I felt a chill within me. The only warmth anywhere radiated from Greta's smile and teary eyes. The television crew seated the three mothers at the front of the audience while microphones were attached and studio lights prepared for Mr. Rivera's entrance.

Geraldo introduced the psychics, giving a synopsis of their experience. Rivera began with questions to Johnny's mother. She answered, handing the psychics a picture of Johnny and a sweater. The psychics touched Johnny's belongings, conferred with each other, and said in a gentle way their belief that Johnny had been murdered shortly after his abduction. Mrs. Goshen sat silent as we went to a commercial break.

Shaun's mother, whispered, "If they say my baby is dead, I don't know what I'll do."

I squeezed her hand. "If so," I said, "I am here."

The psychics held the baby's shoe and pacifier as the audience viewed his photo on the studio screen. "Shaun is alive, taken to be sold for adoption."

His mama wept, "Thank God, my baby is alive."

As another commercial aired, I was emotionally drained, wishing I could leave the set, but it was my turn. The program was almost over, Geraldo's questions came, interrupting my answers to ask more questions. While he talked I saw some favorite photos of Sarah on the TV monitor. More commercials before the psychics handled Sarah's sweater and her picture. John and Greta spoke, "Sarah is dead. She was riding in a car, then gone, dead, nothing." I had heard their prediction in the green room but I swallowed hard. Where did my breath go? I felt a gentle hand holding mine. Geraldo was beside me with a kind smile on his face. In a moment he had come to my side, saying wordlessly what only a caring touch could say.

May 1994

WHEN WHAT SHOULD have been Sarah's graduating class of 1994 at Wayland High was nearing the end of their senior year Christina Markunas, a close friend of Sarah's, phoned me telling me the senior class wanted to dedicate their yearbook to Sarah, would we be agreeable? I was honored that her classmates remembered Sarah eight years after they had known her so briefly in fourth grade. She astounded me with her answer: "Mrs. Pryor, most of us will forget the rest of our classmates, but we will never forget Sarah."

The 1994 Wayland High School Yearbook inscription read:

"Dedicated to Sarah Elizabeth Pryor. Never forget her, just put her in your heart and when you want to see her close your eyes and open your heart and take your favorite time with her and she will be there. That way she will never be gone, but always alive."

—Christina Markunas, Editor

September 1995

AT WORK AT 7:30 a.m. one morning Carroll phoned to say our mother had been taken to Emerson Hospital, next to her residence at River Crest Deaconess. Mom's heart was beating erratically as a result of an anomaly called aortic dissection. The doctors wanted her transported into a Boston hospital where an echo cardiogram could be administered, and treatment options recommended. She needed quiet bed rest in the meantime. I promised to get to the Emerson Hospital as soon as possible, to allow Carroll to go home. I called my co-worker Lou Julian to ask him if he would go with me and provide his support while I was seeing Mom.

When we located my mother's room I sat in the chair close to her bed. I held her hand and identified myself in case she was confused.

"Of course, I know who you are!" she said, but she grew silent and subdued, not like Mom. I reassured her we would find out what was going on with her heart and get it fixed. She nodded and drifted off to sleep.

Back in the car Lou said, "I wonder if she will still be here in the morning." I was having the same thought, yet I tried to remain hopeful.

Early next morning I returned to the hospital, hurrying to her room. I started through the doorway, but stopped, alarmed to see the bed empty, stripped of the linen.

"Oh no," I said. "They didn't call to tell me she died during the night." *Wait a minute, was that her voice I was hearing?*

"I'm over here, dear" She sat upright in a cherry arm chair across the room while a staff member changed the bed linens. I regained my composure, thankful that my own heart was still beating.

A nurse explained they were arranging for her to be taken to Boston's New England Deaconess Hospital where she would be hospitalized overnight. Carroll and Bob had planned to drive to a Boston Symphony performance at Tanglewood in western Massachusetts and spend the night at a bed and breakfast. Meg would come from New York City to join them. I insisted that the family keep that plan, go, enjoy the adventure without worrying. I would stay with Mom, promising to call them if anything changed.

After Mother had been moved to a new room we settled in for the day chatting and joking with each other. Suddenly her mood changed.

"I want to tell you a favorite hymn of mine," she said, "'Children of the Heavenly Father.' I want it played at my funeral."

Silence.

"Are you thinking about *your funeral?*" I asked.

She nodded and said, "I don't want people crying all over the place, I just want someone to tell their favorite funny stories about me, then have a party."

I interrupted her—"What if I tell about the time you complained to me, 'Your son called me *feisty,*' and I told you 'Well, you are feisty!'"

Not missing a beat, she retorted, "Then it must be a good thing!"

We laughed as we remembered other Grandma Peg stories. I had diverted the conversation to put aside my confusion with thoughts of her funeral.

Carroll's phone call interrupted us. They were driving back to Concord and set to arrive within the hour. I gave Mom the update. She sat quietly. What was she thinking? Moments passed. "Will you always remember this day?" I knew a good response to her question since I had read the advice given in the book, *Final Gifts: Understanding the Special Awareness, Needs and Communications of the Dying,* by Maggie Callanan and Patricia Kelley. These Hospice nurses advised families how they might respond better to challenging, often confused, conversations with their loved ones. I remembered to repeat the question asked, then to wait for more information.

Mom asked me, "Will you always remember this day?"

"Yes," I said, "I will always remember this day"

"We had so much fun, didn't we?"

"We did have fun!"

"The three of us had fun!" she said.

"What do you mean, Mom, there are only two of us—you and me!"

"I mean the three of us—you, me, and Sarah!"

"Do you mean because we were talking about Sarah?"

Mom shook her head *no,* abruptly ending our conversation. I knew my question had been off-base, because at that moment Sarah had certainly been in the room for my mom.

Just then Carroll, Bob, and Meg entered the room, smiling as they greeted her. She chirped brightly, "We've been planning the music for my funeral." Carroll and Meg stood speechless. Bob made a hasty retreat out of the room and I attempted to explain what I didn't really understand.

The next morning, I went in the ambulance with Mom for the test. In Boston the EMTs deftly lifted her gurney to the sidewalk. In the bright light of the day I saw she was wearing her big Jackie Onassis sunglasses, looking like a stylish woman on an adventure. When the test results came back to us we sighed with relief. All she needed was a pacemaker to keep her heart at a steady rate. As soon as the pacemaker was implanted Mom was eager to return to her residence. She continued to be a model of hope and enthusiasm for living life, always wearing her favorite lapel pin which read: "Old Age isn't for Sissies."

AN IDEA HAD been brewing in my mind, born from gratitude for the Wayland community which had cared unceasingly about our family. One day, sitting with friends over lunch at work, I realized that Nancy Schon's artist's studio was located within five minutes of my workplace. Nancy is the renowned creator of the sculpture in the Boston Public Garden of the Mallard family from Robert McCloskey's book, *Make Way for Ducklings*. On a whim I called her, identifying myself as Sarah Pryor's mother. We made a plan for me to visit the next day. At the meeting Nancy said that she sculpted animals and had no desire to create a statue of Sarah because, "My sculptures are intentionally designed for children to climb on, saying to children "Please, touch me."

Since she knew little about Sarah's life she asked me to share favorite stories. One memory was of Sarah insisting on sledding early on snowy mornings with her Border Collie, Katie. Before Sarah left for school she put on her snow gear then headed out the door to take a few runs down the little hill in our yard. She delighted in her dog crouched down in front of her, barking loudly and trying without success to herd Sarah, as was the dutiful instinct of a Border Collie. The pair completed several noisy rides, then it was time for Sarah to get ready to walk to school.

She always came in the house soaking wet, needing a change into dry clothes for school. In frustration one day, I admonished her, "Sarah Pryor, you can wait to do your sledding when school is out at 3:00."

Placing her hands on her hips, she replied, "Well, what if the sun comes out today and melts all the snow?" That was the anecdote that inspired Nancy to create a sculpture of Sarah's dog Katie beside an empty sled. I told Nancy what a great idea I thought it was. The sculpture would commemorate Sarah's childhood and the precious gift she gave to all she knew, her wisdom to live each moment fully.

[16] THE JOY OF
CHILDREN

October 9, 1995

OUR FAMILY AND friends gathered with Nancy Schon at the Hannah Williams Park on Route 27 in Wayland to break ground for Nancy's sculpture. It also seemed a good time to have a church service at Trinitarian Congregational Church remembering Sarah after the groundbreaking. Andy and I invited our friend the Rev. David Jones (who spoke after both the ground-breaking and the later dedication) to give the address which follows.

"SARAH IS NOT here, but I am going to presume to tell you a couple of things that I know she would say to us.

"Number One: If there is a lesson in what happened to me, let it be this for you. Live life like a nine-year old on a snowy Saturday morning. Live life joyfully, right up to the edge of your possibilities. Do not waste time being angry, frustrated, depressed, bitter, and preoccupied with things that do not really matter. Little girls on snowy Saturday mornings don't do that. Don't you do it either.

"Number Two: Remember to do your sledding now, not tomorrow. For while today it may be snowing, tomorrow it may not be. Go sledding today. Do you have letters you ought to write somebody? Write them tonight before you go to bed. Do you have phone calls you need to make? Make them today. Do you have people you need to see to straighten some things out with or just to say, "I love you?" Do it now. Do it today and you won't have to worry about tomorrow.

"Number Three: She says, "Cling to one another." You cannot manage things like this all by yourself. It is why we are in this place tonight. And why we have been here for one another these past ten years. Do not try to be a solo, virtuoso performer, all on your own. Cling to one another, just the way she clung to you.

"Number Four: Look up, around, and within to see the face of God. This family has made such an impression upon the Wayland community, upon the people back in Western Pennsylvania, upon all of greater Boston and upon me and my family because they have known how to look into the face of God in the worst experience of their lives. It has been God himself who has carried them through the darkness of the valley of the shadow. She would tell you, "Look up, look around, and look within."

"Number Five: I know Sarah would tell you to take care of the children. She would say to look out for all the little boys and the little girls right now, who can get lost—little ones in school, who are in their homes, who are in places, where it ought to be safe and it isn't. Look out for them, for if you don't no one else will. Your children and my children belong right here-in our hearts. This is where we need to keep them.

"If you and I strive to do these five things that Sarah would tell us, then she will be honored, and she will be pleased. So thank you, Sarah. We know you are all right. Say a prayer for us. We are trying so hard to be all right too."

Barbara and Nancy Schon with a maquette of the Dog and Sled memorial sculpture.

Excerpts from Nancy Schon's book, *Make Way for Nancy: A Life in Public Art* (2017)

"I'VE WRITTEN ABOUT a number of my public art projects, which were commissioned to honor others. What's behind these projects matters to me. Sometimes, even the most atrocious, heinous event can be turned into a peaceful, loving, contemplative environment, one that can bring comfort. Public art has many purposes and touches many people in different ways. Perhaps because I've used animals as metaphors, my sculptures have tended to be positive. But whenever a work honors the memory of a loss—whether of a child or an adult, whether from a horrific event or a drawn-out illness—the making of the work and the story behind it are deeply affecting. I can't bring back the one lost through bronze, but I can, or can try to, create a sculpture that echoes the child's spirit and bring positive thoughts to others, to generations who never knew the departed person.

"So many of the stories behind my sculptures begin with a phone call. This one, in 1995, shook me. When I realized who was calling, I felt a current of deep sympathy rush through me. It was Barbara Pryor, mother of Sarah Pryor, nine years old, who had disappeared ten years previously. She wanted to know what it would take for me to do a sculpture in remembrance of Sarah.

"I invited Barbara to my studio, which at that time was in Wayland, in the same small town in Massachusetts, 40 miles west of Boston, where Sarah died. Barbara and I both were in tears as she told me about the family's move from Pittsburgh, how they were settling in, and about the horrible day, never to be forgotten. Law enforcement agencies and hundreds of volunteers searched the area for weeks, and then months, but found no trace of her.

"She told me how Sarah loved to go sledding before breakfast with her dog Katie, a Border Collie. Once Barbara suggested that Sarah wait until after school to sled. Sarah smiled, put her hands on her hips, and said, "Mom, what if the sun comes out and melts all the snow?"

"The sculpture Barbara wanted was one of a young girl. As we talked, I said gently that experience had shown me that children tend to glance at sculptures of people and move on. But a child will make a parent stop at a sculpture of an animal, to pet or hug or talk to the sculpture. Barbara left me with the thought that we might make something joyful that children could have fun with.

"How might I make a *living memorial* children could interact with? For some reason, I remembered the John F. Kennedy funeral procession with the rider-less horse, a metaphor for Kennedy's absence and death. And I put that together with Sarah's dog Katie.

"This sad mother was willing to try an experiment. She brought a sled from her garage to Hannah Williams Park, a local park, where we hoped the sculpture could go. I brought a friend's dog. At the park, I asked kids to come over to the sled and dog. Barbara, her husband Andrew, and I watched. The kids sat on the sled and played with the dog, which is what I'd hoped. Barbara and Andrew accepted the idea: an empty sled and dog.

"My veterinarian knew of a woman in the area who raised Border Collies, and I met her and took photos. I made a maquette for the Pryors. Barbara became the moving force for raising money from the cultural council and selectmen. For donors, I made a tiny sled to be worn as a pendant or pin, which I cast and finished in gold, with a garnet added, which was Sarah's birthstone.

"With tireless energy and enthusiasm for the sculpture, Barbara, Andrew, their other children, her mother, her work colleagues, her friends, all got out and helped. It was a magnificent show of love and caring. The police and several district attorneys were involved, along with neighbors and businesses who volunteered and contributed."

October 6, 1996

ALMOST ONE YEAR later, in October of 1996, the news reported, "A life-size sculpture memorializes Sarah Pryor at the Hannah Williams Park, Route 27 Wayland. The statue features Sarah's most beloved possessions: her sled and her Border Collie, Katie. Eleven years after Sarah's disappearance, *Dog and Sled* was installed in the Hannah Williams Park, a lovely park with a huge jungle-gym yards away, a nice place for children to meet other children, for mothers to meet, and all to watch after one another."

And Nancy Schon added, "I hope I created a place for the family to come and grieve. But this is not meant to be morbid. We have tried to turn a tremendous tragedy in the past into a future delight."

The sculpture of Sarah's sled and her dog Katie, lovingly crafted by Nancy Schon, was dedicated at a public gathering on that brilliant autumn day. Carroll's oldest son, Rowen, traveled from San Francisco to join our family at this special event. Rowen was talented at writing poetry and graciously granted my request that he create a poem for the occasion. He stepped to the microphone, a hush fell over the crowded park, he began reading the poem he had crafted for the dedication:

I Know Where To Find Her

By Rowen Sandel

My cousin Sarah was taken eleven years ago

And she may be physically missing,

She may have been abducted,

But she is not lost . . . not to me. I know where to find her.

Sarah is anywhere where a pile of leaves calls to you to dive in it.

Sarah is anywhere where a blanket of new-fallen snow asks for you to embrace it. Sarah is anywhere where a field of long swaying grass rises for you to dance and run free in it.

Or anywhere where a sweet new flower opens for you to smell it. Sarah is anywhere where the first instinct is to go and do, not to wait and worry. Sarah is anywhere where a white snow-laden hill offers to trade five minutes of climbing for thirty seconds of wind in your face, excitement, and laughter. She is where children's shrieks and laughter from play can be heard. She is where a barking dog sings a siren's song, calling you to join in, frolic, run free.

Sarah is anywhere and everywhere I go.

And she is anywhere where many of you go.

Sarah is not lost to everyone only to those people who think first of how cold it is outside, and how steep the hill is and how the snow will clutch and cling to their already heavy boots.

Sarah is lost to those people who cannot close their eyes and recapture everything from their youth, their best friend, their favorite stuffed animal, their best sledding hill, their most secret hiding place.

She is lost to those people who cannot laugh or smile, who cannot open their eyes wide to something new and simple like fresh-fallen snow.

Sarah is not lost to me. What was in her, is in me, is in here.

I know where to find her.

Sarah is here in this park and she will always be here. Sarah is here in this statue. This statue will never rust, never wither nor waste away.

It will never grow old and it will never be taken away.

This statue is a reminder, a map even, of where Sarah is.

It will always be here to help people who may feel as if they have lost her.

If you can stand here and watch these children play and listen to them laugh and still you cannot find Sarah, and still you cannot feel Sarah, then it is you that is lost, not Sarah.

Because Sarah is not lost, she is here and here and there and there, and everywhere.

Sarah is not lost.

I know where to find her.

WHEN BECKY OHMAN plays the flute, it becomes part of her. The music flows beautifully through her and soothes my soul. I had asked this musician from my church if she would play a medley of tunes as people gathered for the program. When the ceremony ended I said, "I want to honor children I know about who have gone before us. I believe they are smiling today and thinking of all the children in the future who will play here on the playground and sit on Sarah's dog or sled." Becky played soft background music as I read the names of children who, like Sarah, left our earth too soon:

- Drew Smith, beloved nephew of mine, died at five months
- Cathy Malcolmson, 16, abducted, presumed murdered by Sarah's abductor
- Mark Forti, 9, neighbor, of leukemia
- Louis D. Brown, 15, murdered in cross gunfire, gang violence
- Joanne and Bruce Murphy, sister and brother, 7 and 20, of cystic fibrosis
- Paula Danforth, 19, murder victim
- Holly Piirainen, 10, murder victim
- Sarah Philipps, 20, victim of the terrorist bombing over Lockerbie, Scotland
- Karen Tomyl, 17, of Lupus' complications
- Melissa Benoit, 16, murder victim
- Lacey Parker, 10, drunk driving victim
- Karen Dudley, killed by a drunk driver when she was in college
- Frankie Barnes, murdered at age 10
- Paul Keely, first son to die of unknown illness
- Joe Keely, second son killed by a drunk driver
- Jimmy Keely, third son murdered

Charlie Austin shares his splendid voice at Sarah's sculpture dedication. He also sang at Sarah's grave privately for the family, of which there are no photos. Charlie sang throughout the rain. Byron fell to the ground and exclaimed, "I can't leave you!"

Late October 1996

THE REVEREND DAVID B. Jones gave this "Remembering Sarah" homily at my church, Trinitarian Congregational, on the Sunday after the dedication of Nancy's sculpture:

SARAH REMEMBERED

". . . and a little child shall lead them."

—Isaiah 11:6

"THERE IS A little girl who has led me closer to the Lord over the past year. I have learned a great deal from Sarah Pryor and I am grateful to her and to her family. Several weeks ago, I spoke at a service at Peter's Township, St. David's Church where the Pryor family had worshipped. The church dedicated a stained-glass window in thanksgiving for the life of little Sarah Pryor. I read a quotation from Bishop Hathaway; 'Whether we will someday welcome Sarah home, or whether it will be Sarah who welcomes at our final homecoming, we do not know.'

"Just then, I looked up and saw my own two daughters sitting in the congregation, safe at their mother's side, and I suddenly realized how much Sarah had taught me about gratitude, compassion, and prayer. I cannot count the number of times over this past year I have remembered Sarah when I tucked one of my own children into bed. She taught me about appreciating all of the people the Lord has given to me to love. It has been her ministry to remind others of how much for which we have to be grateful. Let each of us be grateful for what we have, for there is always more to be grateful for than there is to complain about.

"As Sarah's abduction revealed the darkest side of human nature, so did people's response to her disappearance reveal a powerful compassion that is planted deep within us by the Creator. It has been a gift to be reminded of that.

"Finally, there is what Sarah has taught me about prayer. I have never prayed so continually, over such a long period of time in such a focused way, with such a large group of people as I have for Sarah and her family. I have prayed in the shower, at communion, while jogging, mowing the lawn, and on many other diverse occasions. I have discovered the meaning of the phrase, "at all times and in all places" as it relates to prayer.

"'And a little child shall lead them.' Three things I have learned from a nine-year-old. For some much-needed lessons in gratitude, in compassion, and in prayer, thank you, Sarah."

[17] SARAH'S PLACE

D.A. REILLY DEDICATES "SARAH'S PLACE,"
Cambridge, MA: Local Artists, Students, Businesses Volunteer Efforts for Victims of Crime

"Middlesex District Attorney Tom Reilly today dedicated 'Sarah's Place,' which is named in memory of nine-year-old Sarah Pryor. The suite of refurbished rooms was created to provide victims of crime and their families with a safe, private retreat within the criminal justice as their court cases proceed. The unique space with art work and furniture would not have been possible without the generous contributions of local businesses and artists, and individuals who donated furniture, books, art work, and other necessities."

April 18, 1997

THE MIDDLESEX DISTRICT Attorney's office in Cambridge had been working on an idea which delighted me. They wanted to provide a suite of rooms to be dedicated to Sarah and used by victims and their families as a secluded waiting area during court proceedings. Sadly in many courthouses there was no area to be free of the presence of the accused or the media. With my enthusiastic support the work began on the designated space. A local retailer donated the furnishings, our family placed mementoes of Sarah, local artists and elementary school children provided the décor. Since the dedication, victims have waited here during their trial process and have reported finding a peaceful spirit in these rooms I call "Sarah's Safe Haven." A Guest Book has been available to record victims' thoughts. Many have expressed finding peace in the midst of facing the accused in court.

Victims felt protected and grateful that someone cared for them during their stress-filled days. One entry was from a teenager. She wrote, "I am 17 years old and I am here in Sarah's Place awaiting the trial of the man who raped me. I have been so scared to have to face him again, but I know it is the right thing to do. I want to thank you for having this safe place for me and my family to wait. Somehow, I feel peaceful, and this place has given me some courage. Thank you again."

Sarah's Place is a beautiful space. Her spirit lives there, love put into action. I was excited by the entire ribbon-cutting-event. My friend said she was glad I had invited her. She was meant to be there, she declared, her face radiant, then turned with grimace. Her daughter had been raped at about Sarah's age, and many times my friend had been in this building amid de-humanized rooms. She knew how repulsive conditions were then, and what a contrast with the encouragement and peace that these three rooms—filled with paintings, drawings, photos, books, new furniture—now embody.

Later, reflecting on the dedication of Sarah's Place, I thought my Sarah had a short life but her legacy was living on in the hearts of many. There would be countless lives uplifted by my sweet child's spirit.

May 1997

OVER THE YEARS that Sarah was missing, news coverage continued as investigators worked earnestly to find out what happened to our Sarah. Three years after Sarah's suspected abduction Chief of Police Gerry Galvin had said, "We have seven loose leaf notebooks of information on this case, three ring binders, all full."

One evening we watched the local news and saw the familiar face of Gerry Galvin answering questions about the on-going investigation into Sarah's alleged abduction. One of the many binders of Sarah Pryor information was laid out on his desk. When the interview was ending Gerry flipped the binder closed and there was Sarah's sweet picture pasted on the front cover. The Chief looked down at her face, smiled, and said, "That's my girl, that's my girl." Meg and I both wept tears of deep gratitude when we heard Gerry's comment.

June 1997

ONE SUNNY AFTERNOON in early June a call came from District Attorney Tom Reilly. "We have assembled critical Sarah data as we continue working on Sarah's case. We have her fingerprints and her dental charts. But with today's current DNA technologies it may be necessary for us to get a blood sample from you. You have respected the investigative team's work, always being aware of the need for confidentiality. I need to let you know a man was walking his dog near woods in the area. The dog discovered what appeared to be human remains."

Peter Sennett, from the DA's office, was watching a Discovery Channel program with his kids when the forensic anthropologist who discovered the highly technical mitochondrial testing of bones appeared. William C. Rodriquez, III of the Armed Forces Institute of Pathology in Washington, D.C. explained the new technology. Tom Reilly had phoned Dr. Rodriquez to ask if he would take Sarah's case. He agreed saying it was a long-standing open case of a missing child. Lab tests would determine if the bone was Sarah's. If they found distinct markings in the bone I would need to donate a vial of my O-positive blood as children carry unique DNA from their mother. Tom asked that I guard the information he had just divulged telling no one else.

I respected Tom's wishes for confidentiality, but I knew I must share the burden of the startling news with Carroll and Bob. I arrived at their house and the three of us drove all over the town on an amateur detective mission looking for recent construction sites where the remains might have been discovered. We felt we were doing something useful during the outing although in the end we were clueless about the location.

The morning after that adventure I awoke with a painful headache, certain I had a bad case of sinusitis. A quick appointment and diagnosis from my primary care physician got me started on prescribed medication. I felt as if a tractor trailer was parked on my face. The pain radiated from my eye sockets down to my jaw line. Even with a powerful antibiotic, I felt little relief from the throbbing pain. Post-traumatic stress had come with the news of the bone fragment. Probably I had accepted the fact that I would never know for sure what had happened to Sarah. Now it was quite possible we might find out something. I tried to stay in the present, not imagining what the tests would tell, but my body reacted with this severe sinus infection after the long years of not knowing.

Two days later I met with the church women's monthly Hospitality Committee. We provided food and fellowship after church service on Sunday mornings. I enjoyed my work with the other members who were fun, diverse, and eager to serve. Prayer time was essential at the end of our meetings and I requested healing of my sinus infection, then reminded the women that although I could not divulge what was happening their prayers were needed for the investigators working on Sarah's case. As most of the women departed Janet, my fashionable "sixty-something" friend, approached me with a whisper asking, "Do you know what is going on in the investigation?"

I answered politely, "Yes, but I cannot talk about it."

Janet surprised me, "We need to step outside so that we can talk privately."

Leading me away from the other women, she said "Barbara, they found the bone on my property more than a year ago." She owned a sizable piece of land on Route 20, near the intersection of Route 26, where she stabled horses just two miles from our home on Concord Road. I assumed her private farm property had not been included in the search in 1985 after Sarah was missing, because the police had concentrated on public land. In recent years the land around her property had been developed and houses now surrounded the horse farm. I was glad that my friend had honored the investigators' request for confidentiality, being quietly cooperative showing her property to anthropologists and other members of the law enforcement community for a year as they tried to find more remains and identify the bone. The DNA specialists said they thought the bone belonged to a female who was likely thirteen or fourteen years old. (Remember Sarah was 5 feet, 2 inches, tall for her age.)

Later that afternoon Janet walked with me to show me the grounds where the intensive search had taken place. Only a jaw bone was found, although the investigative team had searched for months before cold weather set in. Sarah had not been buried in the woods; thus animals were able to scatter her remains. The cruel reality set into my mind, washing over me in sobs that I thought would not end.

September 1997

WHILE I WAITED to learn more about the DNA testing an event happened which kept my mind from wandering to thoughts of what might have happened to Sarah. I had a horrific fall in my apartment when my arthritic knee buckled at the top of the staircase on the second floor and I pitched head-first down fourteen uncarpeted wooden steps. I was out of my body, peacefully noting that this was an interesting way to be going down the stairs. I felt no pain, had no fear, but instead felt suspended in the air for what seemed like twenty minutes or more. Although my landlady heard me screaming I did not hear or feel anything. Not until I landed in a heap at the bottom of the staircase did my body connect again to my conscious mind.

An ambulance rushed me to our local hospital in a brace for fear of a broken neck. Thankfully x-rays showed no broken bones although my lacerated chin needed seven stitches. My body soon showed the evidence of the sudden fall as my face, arms, and legs turned black and blue and I looked as though I had been physically abused. It took weeks to recover with physical and water therapy so that I was distracted while waiting to hear the lab results by focusing on healing my bruised and hurting body.

The trauma of the fall on the stairs reminded me of the wise counsel of Hillary Bercovicci, a seminary student assigned some years ago to our church in Pennsylvania. He had the true gift of pastoral counseling and offered his time to church members who wanted to speak to him privately. I was struggling with personal issues and sought his aid to help sort out my feelings. He challenged my thinking that other people had much worse pain than mine. He gently yet firmly countered, "There is no scale that measures the weight of pain. Pain is pain is pain. If you've known pain, you can relate to anyone's pain." Initially I had rejected that thought, but the idea took root and the possibility of its truth began to grow in my mind.

Hillary phoned me from his Maryland home when he heard that Sarah was missing. I was surprised, but very glad of the call. I shared with him that I was afraid to think of the possibility that Sarah was suffering or that she was no longer alive.

He told me about his own near-death experience while an EMT in New York City. He had been attacked by a gang, and while being brutally beaten he experienced an out-of-body feeling, looking down from a height and observing what was happening to him. I held securely to this hope. Perhaps Sarah had been protected from feeling fear and pain. In a strange way I was thankful for the fall down stairs as it helped me remember Hillary's experience and advice.

When a well-intentioned person says to me, "Your loss, the murder of a child, is the worst," I am uncomfortable because I think of Hillary and his statement about the quality of pain, viewing my pain as not more or less than another's but rather as a key to connect with another's burden.

November 1997

A WEEK BEFORE Thanksgiving I wanted to find out what was taking so long to hear the DNA results. I talked with one of the Middlesex Assistant district attorneys, John McEvoy. He chuckled, "I always said your instincts are so on target we should have you on the team! We just received feedback and there are distinct markings which will give definite answers once we have your blood sample. Although it isn't necessary it would be helpful if either Meg or Byron would give a sample too, if they are home for Thanksgiving." I told him I would arrange for my blood to be drawn at my family health center and would ask Meg to give a sample as well. Peter Sennett would be at the appointment to take the samples from Boston to Virginia for the analysis. John said we should have an answer fairly quickly thereafter. I thanked John and added that Andy and I agreed that we did not want to hear the results until after Christmas.

My major concern was asking Meg to give a blood sample without triggering her fears that her sister was not alive. Tom Reilly provided helpful advice: "I would tell her with modern technology the blood samples are a necessary routine in the investigation. You should tell her that we are working on a lead presently or she might feel betrayed if it turns out to be a positive identification." Grateful for his advice but nervous, I asked Meg to go with me to dinner at a local restaurant for food and quiet time to talk. We ordered beverages and appetizers. The waiter left to place the order and I casually mentioned that Tom and I had talked recently by phone. Meg respected and trusted him and asked about the conversation. I repeated what Tom had scripted for me. Meg said, "I have one question—will the blood work hurt?"

Relieved, I said, "Only for a moment!"

A day or two later our bloods were drawn. We greeted Peter Sennett who signed for and received the samples and left the health center for a latte and scone at a coffee shop. Meg's holiday visit was soon over, it was time for me to drive her to the bus back to New York University in Manhattan. I waited with her on a bench, noticing my usually bubbly, talkative Meg was quiet. I surmised she did not want to talk about the blood tests. Meg knew if she asked me any question, I would give her an honest answer. I hugged her as the bus approached saying, "See you very soon for your Christmas vacation."

I sat for a while wondering what was going through her mind.

PART FOUR:
FAREWELL

[18] NEWS

JANUARY 10 WAS a wintery day, grey and blustery. I parked my car saying to myself, *This is the day all the years of wishing and waiting will end.* At 4:00 p.m. that afternoon Tom Reilly called to say the bone fragment was a positive identification. The Sarah Investigation Team would need to meet with Andy and me as soon as possible. The abrupt news was too much for me to take in. My friends and co-workers Julie and Lee were seated with me when Tom broke the news. I could barely breathe, let alone think what had to be done. I needed time to process the end to the years of waiting. Tom, concerned for my driving in that state of mind, said he would send Peter Sennett to drive me to Cambridge to meet at the DA's office with Andy, and the dedicated team who had worked so hard to find answers about Sarah. Julie and Lee left the room to tell Jonathan, our office manager, the confidential news. He asked what I most needed. My friends said, "Us, Barbara needs *us* by her side."

Jonathan said, "Go and stay with her."

In Cambridge at the District Attorney's office we gathered in a conference room. Tom began "This is the day we have waited for. After long years, we now have an answer. It is a sad day for all of us." He explained mitochondrial DNA testing and that there was no doubt the bone belonged to Sarah. He suggested that we move from the conference room to the dedicated suite of rooms called Sarah's Place. Tom offered a short prayer then told us Dr. Rodriquez would travel to Boston with the bone fragment and verify Sarah's death to the County Coroner. Our family could finally plan a funeral for Sarah.

We were grateful for the years of concern the public had shared for Sarah and with our family since her abduction. Many people worried and waited with us, but confidentiality was extremely important to prevent a leak to the media. The question was how to tell the news to out-of-state family members. Meg was touring in the cast of *Damn Yankees*, currently performing in Chicago. Byron and Jennifer had been married in June and moved to Gambier, Ohio, where Byron worked in campus ministry at Kenyon College, and Jennifer was employed as a registered nurse in the Geriatric Unit at Knox Hospital. Last on my list was my father who was hospitalized in the Pittsburgh, PA, area. I would talk personally with Mother at her assisted living place.

I called Carroll at work asking if Bob would come to the court house, then drive me to their house where I could stay protected from the media. There I made my first call to Meg. She answered on the first ring.

"Hi, sweetie it's Mom. I have some news to tell you but I need to know that your roommate Ashley is with you."

Meg asked, "Why? What's wrong? What's happened?"

"Meg, before I tell, you I need to know that someone is with you." I feared hearing the news about her sister would send her emotions spinning out of control. I started gently, "Tom Reilly has called with sad news; the investigators have positively identified a bone fragment as belonging to Sarah. That means that we will need you to come home for a funeral next week."

She screamed, sending chills through me, then said "I can't talk about this—no, I have to take this in. I'll call you back."

Before I hung up I talked to Ashley to be sure she would stay with Meg.

When I dialed Byron and Jennifer's number her cheery voice greeted me. I began, "Is Byron at home with you?"

"No, he's been helping coach basketball at an away game for Kenyon. Why?"

I continued, "I have some sad news to tell both of you but I want you to go get your neighbor to be with you after I tell you. Then you will need to have someone drive to the game to tell Byron."

Jen assured me she would go to their neighbor after I told her the news. Although my daughter-in-law had never known Sarah she loved her. I heard sobbing so intense I worried Jen could not breathe. I hated not being with my dear ones to put my arms around them. Jennifer rallied, then switched to her emergency nurse mode formulating a plan to notify Byron. She would ask their minister to travel to the basketball game to tell him.

My eighty-eight-year-old father was hospitalized in Washington, PA, for congestive heart failure. D.H. Smith had been a successful business man with a take-charge nature that had been stymied by Sarah's unsolved case. Although Dad was lucid and capable of conversation I wanted to be cautious talking with him. His cardiologist,

Dr. John Frazier, suggested Dad have a friend in the room when I telephoned with the news. I dialed the hospital room and asked, "How are you doing, Dad?"

His joking answer, "Lousy, how are you?"

In a serious voice I told him about the bone identification. His reaction was different from Meg and Jen. He wanted to know every detail about where, how, and when they had found the bone.

I realized that he was tiring and ended the conversation with, "I'll be in touch. In the meantime, we need to keep the news tightly wrapped," meaning it was to be held in confidence. Dad didn't understand my "keep it confidential" message and relayed my news to the friend sitting with him. The next day Dad's friend shared the news with the morning coffee klatch of community leaders including the editor of the local newspaper.

Once the news of the identification of Sarah's bone became public in my small hometown it moved with lighting speed from Washington, Pennsylvania, to Boston and New England prompting an immediate media frenzy. My landlady called the local police to get rid of a reporter who was harassing her for information about where he could locate me. The evening news was filled with speculation and half-truths while I was safely in hiding at Carroll's. What lay ahead of me was formidable. I had a funeral to plan, family to transport from the airport, and a press conference to deliver.

There was one more person to tell about Sarah, my Mom. Physically and emotionally exhausted from the three calls I had already made, I knew I could depend on Carroll for her strength. "If I go to Mom's with you, will you please do the talking?" I knew Carroll would do it for me.

Saturday, January 10, 1998

Barbara Pryor's Press Statement

"Our hearts have felt for some time that Sarah has been in heaven. Now, with the positive identification of Sarah's remains, we have conclusive proof which confirms it. Over the past 12 years, we have been truly blessed to have had a team of competent, dedicated, and caring investigators who simply did not give up. They have found her.

"Additionally, none of us could have handled the roller coaster of these last years without the support, prayers, and love of countless New Englanders. We know that you, the members of the media, have also cared and been concerned about Sarah and her family. Thank you. We ask you now to abide by our wishes that you give us private time to plan her funeral and burial. Nothing comes to mind that better describes Sarah's spirit than what is written in Paul's letter to the Colossians, Chapter 3, verse 12: "Dearly beloved, clothe yourselves with compassion, kindness, humility, gentleness, and patience. Bear with each other and forgive whatever grievances you may have against each other. Forgive as the Lord forgives. And over all these virtues put on love, which binds them all together.""

"I ask you now to direct your focus to honoring the beautiful spirit of our precious Sarah. Let us love one another and bind ourselves together in that love. We will get through this together. Now, please go home and hug your children and tell them that you love them."

Sunday, January 11, 1998

The next day the *Middlesex News* reported, "SARAH PRYOR'S REMAINS IDENTIFIED. On Saturday, January 10, 1998 family, friends and investigators on the 'Sarah Team' gathered for a press conference on the lawn of the Wayland Police Department."

Tom Reilly had introduced Dr. Rodriguez who explained the DNA findings. The funeral schedule was in place; visitation hours would be open to the public on Monday, January 12th at Trinitarian Congregational Church, a block from where we were standing for the press conference. Sarah's funeral would follow on Tuesday, January 13, with burial immediately following at the Lakeview Cemetery in Wayland. January 13th would have been Sarah's 22nd birthday.

In the report, Wayland Police Chief, Gerald Galvin, who was the lead investigator in the case when Sarah disappeared on October 9th, 1985, said, "When the results came back last week, they unlocked the mystery of Pryor's disappearance . . . We're closing one chapter of the investigation, but it opens another."

It was all over the news:

"I am here to tell you that we have identified a portion of the remains of Sarah Pryor," said (Tom) Reilly, who arrived at the (police) station wearing muddy boots after a visit to the (Wayland) woods of Blossom Lane where the remains were found. Sarah may not have gotten more than a few miles from home."

—*Boston Sunday Herald*, January 11, 1998

New Way to Analyze DNA a Proven Success

"Peace for the family of Sarah Pryor at last has been assured through a little-known process of DNA analysis. Studied by medical researchers since 1981, mitochondrial DNA analysis has seen more general use only since 1991 when the military began employing it to identify American servicemen's bones on former battlefields of Vietnam, Korea, and Europe. For families with missing relatives, the practice has provided hope where standard (nuclear) DNA testing could not. The much larger quantity of DNA strands gives investigators a better chance that some will be preserved, even after years . . . mothers pass the DNA to all of their children, so investigators in the Pryor case were able to compare the skull fragment's mitochondrial DNA with that of Pryor's mother, Barbara, and Sarah's sister, Meg."

—*Boston Sunday Herald*, January 11, 1998

Complicated tests used to identify Pryor

"On Friday, two days after his DNA tests on a skull fragment ended the decade-long search for Sarah Pryor, Dr. William Rodriguez left his Maryland Armed Forces Institute of Pathology and boarded a plane bound for Boston. Touched by the bravery of Pryor's parents, he wanted to personally meet them and return their daughter's remains. "I have children of my own," he said. 'I can't imagine what it would be like to lose one of them.'"

—*The Middlesex News,* Wayland

January 12, 1998, by Michael Kunzelman

When Science Brings a Family Relief

"Pryor's case was one of only a few chosen from hundreds of law enforcement request sent to the Armed Forces Institute of Pathology in Washington, DC, during the last two years seeking the expensive, highly technical mitochondrial DNA testing. "We chose Sarah's case because it was unique, it was old, there were very little remains," said forensic anthropologist, William C. Rodriguez III, head of the Armed Forces DNA Identification Laboratory in Rockville, MD, which did the actual testing. 'Closure is a great relief, and that is what we can bring," said Rodriguez.'"

—*The Boston Globe* January 12, 1998

[19] SARAH'S FAREWELL

IN THE YEARS after Sarah's abduction several mental health professionals helped me deal with long-term grief. Waiting for the Army lab to identify the skeletal remain was difficult to bear, especially with the burden of maintaining confidentiality. My grief counselor suggested that I plan a funeral service rather than a memorial service in the event the test results proved positive. This would give everyone an opportunity to mourn as well as bring an end to one stage of mourning.

Planning the funeral was heart-wrenching. The public would be invited to afternoon and evening visitation hours at Trinitarian Congregational Church. I imagined there could be a long line of well-wishers and asked that the church parlor be set aside for Sarah's family to greet guests. We planned a route through the church leading well-wishers past her closed casket, then to a storyboard of Sarah photos. A short video of Sarah at her teacher's wedding played in a loop at the beginning of the family receiving line.

Constant companions Julie and Lee took notes as we talked with the minister Dr. Carl Saylor about the funeral service. I asked my family members to decide if they wished to participate, clearly making the choice theirs. Byron chose to read a favorite scripture, Meg a poem, Carroll would say prayers, and Sarah's boy cousins would be pall-bearers for the small white coffin. Andy and I would share special Sarah moments. Carl would officiate. Andy asked a family friend, Reverend David Jones, to join Dr. Saylor with a short homily. When I could no longer concentrate on the planning I excused myself to find solitude in any quiet corner I could find.

The funeral director, Bill Hayes, was a true gift in my hour of need, taking charge of the casket and the burial plot. Because the bone used for DNA identification was so small Bill said there was room for the family to put mementos into the casket to be buried with her. Jen and Byron placed an invitation to their wedding, Meg gave Sarah's Christmas stocking, and others added treasures. I placed a love letter to my dear child.

Bill Hayes suggested that we consider inviting one television station to televise the service. That station could share with other TV outlets so that viewers in New England could feel part of the farewell to the girl they had learned about when she went missing. We chose WCVB Channel 5 because the two anchors, Natalie Jacobson and Chet Curtis, had been particularly thoughtful in interactions with us. We asked that they manage the details, and the service be filmed without lights that might distract from the ceremony. At the end of the service for Sarah, WCVB gave our family video tapes of the celebration of our little girl's short life.

"As you know, Sarah was taken in October of 1985. Since then, we have made literally hundreds of good and caring friends who have supported us through what can only be described as a horrendous nightmare."

—Andrew Pryor, *Boston Sunday Herald*

January 11, 1998

Monday, January 12, 1998
Visitation Hours

PEOPLE GATHERED FOR visitation hours on Monday, the day before Sarah's funeral, standing patiently in a long line from the double doors of the church to greet Andy and me in the parlor. Wayland police officers provided traffic control and directed the hundreds of mourners to enter through the church's main doors to proceed past the small white casket covered with daisy arrangements from the criminal justice team, the church, family members, and friends. Then visitors moved from the sanctuary past a picture board and the short video of Sarah, and into the church parlor where our family gathered. I greeted people and then introduced them to Andy. Meg and Byron stood with relatives off to the side so that they could talk when friends entered the room.

A young woman introduced herself as a new reporter offering her condolences, and asked, "Did you get my telephone message?"

Puzzled, I asked, "What message?"

"I left you a message saying I wanted to interview you before your daughter's funeral tomorrow."

In a quiet, but very firm voice I heard myself say, "I am greeting many people who have come to pay respects to Sarah and her family. This is not the time or the place to be having this conversation. Thank you for coming," then passed her quickly on to Andy while I turned to the next person in line.

A few moments later three girls approached me, the girl in front saying she hoped it was okay that they came even though they did not know us. She reached for my hand and said, "I made these stuffed felt hearts for you, your son and daughter. Whenever you miss Sarah you just squeeze the hearts!"

Somehow, I found my voice, then pulled her to me in a warm hug, thanking her with tears filling my eyes. Three loving girls who brought me needed joy in a sorrowful moment. I carefully placed the hearts in my pocket and made sure to share this gift of love with Byron, Jen, and Meg.

Tuesday, January 13, 1998, Sarah's Funeral

SARAH ELIZABETH PRYOR was born on January 13th in 1976. The day of her funeral, she should have been twenty-two years old. How disturbing to realize I would ever after remember her birthday and funeral on the same day.

That morning I awoke in the guest room in Carroll's house, stretched my legs and arms, then remembered the funeral later in the day. My usual morning eagerness was replaced with gloomy dread. Suddenly the voices of Meg and her girl cousins came wafting up to the second floor laughing and bantering in the kitchen below me. Megan and Kate and Meg loved being together whenever they could. Today was no exception. They were having a good time. How dare they?

I was in a more somber mood. I couldn't bear them having fun. Not today. Certainly not today! I managed to stay upstairs, fuming and fussing, talking to myself as I showered and dressed for the funeral. I refused to wear black but instead decided to wear a new royal blue suit. Sarah had loved bright colors so I added a multicolored scarf. All dressed and prepared now to join the other relatives who had gathered, I went downstairs to discover my female relatives all in black dresses.

"I really can't stand that you all are wearing black! Sarah loved colors!" I blurted.

Carroll calmed my outburst with patience saying, "I have tons of scarves; we'll each pick one to wear for you."

The funeral home sent a limo to pick up Andy, Meg, Byron, Jen, and me to travel from Concord to Wayland. As the limo pulled into the church driveway, a handful of reporters crowded the car. Meg demanded, "Make them go away, Mom!"

I told the driver we would not leave the car until the crowd backed off. He dealt with the reporters and we entered the church. I spotted a church friend and asked her to bring a glass of water and a paper bag. Meg was hyperventilating.

Prayers

WHEN THE FUNERAL was finally underway, prayers and poems and goodbyes were shared by my ex-husband Andy, by me, by Sarah's brother Byron, by her sister-in-law Jennifer, by Sarah's sister Meg, and by her Aunt Carroll. Reverend David Jones shared a homily. My minister, Dr. Saylor, had the hardest task of his life in officiating at Sarah's funeral. These are some excerpts of those wishes:

Andy (Sarah's Father):

"To Sarah, my beautiful daughter. You are with me constantly. I see you whenever I see a father and daughter walking or playing together. I also see you when I see a young girl dancing, jumping, or running in the park. You are with me whenever I feel the joy of life. I am proud to be your father.

"With all my love, your father."

Byron (Sarah's Brother)

"To my sister Sarah: The beautiful baby I ran home to see daily. You were the fuzzy haired "Woodstock" who happily bounced on our back porch; "the blondie" who loved to dance, to swim, and most of all to mimic her big sister Meg. When you started in elementary school you were awkward and shy. I had the privilege as your brother, seven years older than you, to talk with you and try to help you through those difficult times.

"I value memories of your smile, your tears on my shoulder, your laugh, and your love. I will share you with my wife, her family and those who enter my life, and the children who will come. And I long for the day when I will be reunited with you in heaven and hold you again.

"Love, Byron"

Jennifer (Sarah's Sister-In-Law)

"Sarah, I am the sister-in-law you never got to meet. And yet, though I know you only through pictures and stories, I love you, and hold you in a special place in my heart. You wouldn't believe how many people have gathered to tell you good-bye. I am amazed at the impact our shy Sarah had not just on her family but on the community at large. There are so many circumstances surrounding our loss of you that I do not understand, but I do know for sure that in your brief time here with us you gave us love, you experienced love and now it is with love that we bring you to your final resting place. My good-bye is temporary because I will see you in heaven where we will embrace."

Sarah's sister Meg read this poem by Edgar Guest, English-born American poet 1881- 1959:

MISSING SARAH PRYOR

To All Parents

"I'll lend you for a little time
a child of mine," He said.
For you to love the while she lives
and mourn for when she is dead.
It may be six or seven years
or twenty – two or three,
But will you, 'til I call her back,
take care of her for me?
She'll bring her charms to gladden you,
and shall her stay be brief,
You'll have her memories
as solace for your grief.
I cannot promise that she'll stay,
since all from earth return,
But there are lessons taught down there
that I want this child to learn.
I've looked the whole world over
in my search for teachers true,
And from the throngs that crowd life's lanes
I have selected you.
Now will you give her all your love,
nor think the labor vain,
Nor hate me when I come to call
and take her back again?
I fancied that I heard them say,

"Dear Lord, Thy will be done."

For all the joy Thy child shall bring,

the risk of grief we'll run."

We'll shower her with tenderness;

we'll love her while we may,

And for the happiness we've known

forever grateful stay.

But shall the angels call for her

much sooner than we planned,

We'll brave the bitter grief that comes

and try to understand."

Sarah's Aunt Carroll Sandel created and read the Prayers of the Faithful

We Pray To The Lord

"For Andy, Barbara, Byron, Meg and Jen. For her grandparents Dave and Peg, for all the aunts, uncles, and cousins that they continue to grow in God's grace so that through them all will continue to experience the love Sarah shared with them and the world.

"For the children who were Sarah's classmates and friends at Pleasant Valley and Claypit Hill Elementary Schools, who played dress-up and "Barbies," joined her swimming, at sleep-overs and at Indian Princesses. Let her joy, excitement and laughter permanently touch your lives and you use it to grow in God's love.

"For the team of competent, compassionate and dedicated investigators who have relentlessly pursued their mission to bring resolution. We are grateful for your professionalism and kindness. May their virtues of fairness and devotion in the search for Sarah inspire us.

"For the many caring people who never had the joy of knowing Sarah, including the hundreds who first searched for her and those who through the years have been steadfast in their nurturing of Barbara, Andy, Meg and Byron.

"For the Sarah Pryor Memorial Committee and for Nancy Schon who together gave the town a perfect tribute to Sarah at the Hannah Williams Park. May all these wondrous blessings continue to spread and touch our lives.

"Hear our Prayers, O Lord!"

And Sarah's cousin Megan summarized three things she had learned about living with the loss of Sarah.

"First, I realize your time here on this earth can be much shorter than you think, and you should use it to your utmost.

"Second, that if Sarah can touch people's lives she's never met then I have no excuse, not to try and make a difference in everybody's life that I encounter.

"Third, this is just as much about what is good in people as what is evil."

[20] ELEGIES

el·e·gy /ˈeləjē/ noun

1. a poem of serious reflection, typically a lament for the dead.

I shared the following elegy to my beloved daughter, Sarah:

My Elegy for Sarah

A LITTLE AFTER midnight, Sarah Pryor graced us with her presence. Cleaned and wrapped in the hospital new-born blanket, she slept peacefully on my stomach, her daddy nearby. Sarah was bonded to our hearts forever. I want you who didn't know Sarah personally to have a mother's snapshot of her. Most importantly I'd like you to learn life lessons Sarah taught me that you might understand and emulate.

Sarah was a long, lanky kid and she was bald. When her hair came in, it didn't cooperate. It often stuck straight up, cowlicks everywhere. I confess I used hair gel to hold them down. I look at a picture of Sarah as a toddler, posed with her older brother and sister in a studio portrait, and only I know that I had taped a pretty bow on her unruly hair. Her hair did grow into a beautiful ash-blonde. I fondly remember Sarah in yellow-legged pajamas, hair sticking out on either side looking like the comic-strip bird Woodstock!

She was a contented child although she was shy in the company of less familiar folks. Meg was five years old and Byron was seven when Sarah was born. As a former speech therapist, I told the children we were not going to engage in baby talk ("How's our 'wittle' girl?"). They followed my instructions and soon Sarah was imitating her brother and sister.

Sarah was tall for her age and had been reading at age five. Her nursery school teachers recommended she skip kindergarten. Before school started she was tested for her language development which revealed Sarah had the vocabulary and language of an 8th-grader. Here I am, bragging on my kid! As a new 1st-grader Sarah was attending speech class, as she struggled with the "r" sound, a challenge for a girl named "Sarah Pryor!"

Bouncy and enthusiastic, yet needing to be close to her mom, that was my little girl. Whether we were going to the grocery store or going on vacation she was excited. Her sense of humor was unique. One day she arrived home from school carrying a torn jacket. When I asked what had happened she said, "The boys were teasing me." I explained, "Boys often tease girls when they like them." Sarah looked at me with the face of one who cannot believe what was just uttered. "That's the strangest thing I've ever heard!"

Sarah adored being in the swimming pool, armed with her "water wings." She soon tired of the baby area at our community swimming pool, insisting she was big enough for the adult section. I agreed to help her by treading water in the deep end of the pool, catching her as she jumped from the low dive. The lifeguard abruptly ended our fun, cautioning me that this was not a safe procedure as she could inadvertently jump on me. Sarah was not happy when I told her she was to return to the baby pool, or to the part of the pool where she could touch bottom. Thinking the issue was settled I relaxed and chatted with friends. Moments had passed. When I suddenly heard shouts, "Go! Go!" I looked up to the source of the commotion. Sarah was at the edge of the high dive, without her water wings, ready to jump. When I yelled, "What on earth are you doing?" Her simple answer was, "You told me to take off my water-wings!"

When she was four-years-old, I said she could play with her toys . . . as long as she put them all away. As you can guess, they were strewn over the floor. She had merrily trotted off to her bedroom. I loudly called her full name, "Sarah Elizabeth Pryor, come to the head of the stairs."

She appeared, listened to my scolding, then promptly put her hands on her ears announcing, in a volume equal to mine, "I can't hear what you are saying." That statement may have worked with her brother and sister, but not with her mother.

Her compassionate heart cared for those who were hurting. Every year when the Christmas story of Rudolph the Red-Nosed Reindeer aired on television, Sarah would sob, "They aren't being nice to Rudolph." We decided to avoid watching that program.

Sarah loved the snow. On wintery mornings, she would don her snow gear, and head out with her dog, Katie, to take a few sled rides before she left for school. She'd laugh and yell in sheer delight, with her dog barking in hot pursuit. After a few runs, a soaked Sarah would return to the house to change clothes for school. One day in sheer frustration, I said, "Sarah you can wait until after school to do your sledding."

"Mom," she said, "what if the sun comes out today and melts the snow?" I was amazed at her childish desire to live each moment fully.

Many people have long lives and never live well. Sarah Pryor lived her life, short as it was, with gentleness, kindness, playfulness, wisdom, curiosity, gusto, optimism, trust, faithfulness, and most of all with love. Sarah simply did not know hate. She only knew how to love. I hope you see Sarah in me. If you don't, I ask you to remind me that I am not being like my dear child. I've changed the way I live my life, with God's grace, because of Sarah and the life she lived.

She is teaching us, she is beseeching us to cling to each other, let us bind ourselves together in love.

Reflections by Evy Davis

EVY DAVIS is a long-time friend of my sister Carroll's. Evy calls Carroll and me by our childhood nicknames. Carroll is *Gussie* and I am *Babs*. Evy wrote to me, "I was very moved by Sarah's funeral today and only hope that it helped you and the rest of your family. It clearly stirred up feelings for me and so, as I often do I sat down to write about them, so I enclosed them. Love, Evy"

"Today is Sarah Pryor's birthday. Who is Sarah Pryor, you ask? Well, if you don't live in the Northeast you probably don't know. But, Sarah Pryor was a young, playful girl when she was abducted 12 years, 3 months and 4 days ago at the age of 9. Today Sarah should have turned 22 because today is Sarah's birthday. Sarah Pryor is also the niece of my closest friend, Gussie Sandel. I remember well the beautiful October day in 1985 when I was driving home from supervising some of my staff in Springfield, MA, and heard over the radio that Sarah Pryor was missing. What did they mean, *missing*? Certainly, she had just gotten lost, walking in a neighborhood that was still somewhat unfamiliar to her. Of course, we, the adult community who protect our children, would find her and bring her home safely. But large numbers of people searched the neighborhood, the town, the state, and throughout the country, and Sarah was not found. Minutes passed into hours, hours became days, days became weeks, weeks—months, and yes, months have turned into years and Sarah was not found.

"Over the years I have been with the Sandels and Pryors throughout this ordeal. I was at Babs' and Andy's house the night Sarah disappeared and for many subsequent days and nights thereafter. A year after she disappeared I attended the service in her honor at the Pryor's Wayland church. I was at the groundbreaking for the memorial to be built in a Wayland park. I attended the fundraiser for the statue that was being planned. And, finally, 11 years after her disappearance, I attended the unveiling of the bronze sled and dog, 'Sarah's Place,' and gave what I thought would be my final farewell to Sarah Pryor. I felt like I, personally, had completed my mourning. Sarah was gone and I felt as if we had all said, 'Goodbye.'

"Yet, Sarah was not found.

"Eight days ago Gussie called me to say, 'Sarah has been found.' Through highly technical DNA studies a laboratory in Maryland was able to positively identify that some bones found by a dog in a field in Wayland were indisputably Sarah's. The remains, at the time of our telephone conversation, were in Maryland. Babs was going to plan a funeral for when they were returned to the family.

"I had a strong, personal reaction. I thought that the funeral and any ceremonies should be private family affairs. I assumed that the community had, as I had, already put Sarah to rest. But Babs apparently felt that she owed it to the people who had stood by them for so many years to give them one more opportunity to say, 'Good-bye,' and that the community would respond. Clearly, I had underestimated the impact that the Pryors and Sarah had made over the past 12-plus years.

"So yesterday I went to the wake so that I could give support to my close friend, Gussie, and her extended family. I went so that I could be there for the Sandel children whom I love dearly. I went so that I could be there for Meg Pryor who is a part of our extended family. In short, I went for the living. I felt clear that I had put Sarah to rest. I was stunned by the crowd. Policemen directed traffic. Parking attendants assisted drivers in finding a space in the large lot behind the church. On entering the church, many milled around, watching a video of Sarah and looking at bulletin boards of pictures portraying her short life.

"I stood in a long line for a long time to merely have the opportunity to give family members a hug. I waited and I watched. I watched people cry. I watched people hugging. I watched people moved. In short, I was watching love in action. I watched and I wondered—how and why did this little girl and this family touch so many people's lives? I still have no clear answer about that, but I know for a fact it is what has happened.

"I spent the evening talking to a family I, too, love. Not because I was drawn to them because a little girl was abducted and murdered, but because I have known them for 30 years, we have raised our children together, we have spent holidays together and we have shared life's strife and triumphs together. I even risked telling some of them that I thought the huge wake, the publicity, the 'event' was too much. But out of respect and consideration to Andy, Babs, their children, and Gussie, I wanted to be there and offer my support.

"I left work this morning with plenty of time to get to the church early. I did not want to be part of the overflow crowd that had to watch the funeral via video in a nearby church or social hall. I wanted to be "in" the church where the family was. Despite arriving 45 minutes before the service was to begin there was no parking available at the church and I was redirected by one of the many policemen on duty to a nearby town lot. Television cameras abounded. People were streaming into the church. I sat, quietly, towards the back. I did not see a familiar face. And, listening to conversations, it was clear that I knew the family better than those around me. I sat. I waited. I almost had the attitude that I was just at another of my day's appointments— my 11 a.m. to 1 p.m. activity on Tuesday, January 13, 1998. I quickly learned that this was far from just 'another appointment.'

"Following some beautiful flute and piano music the service began. Psalms, poems, hymns, remembrances, family members—it had the spirit of memory, of celebration, of recalling a young girl—her delights, her annoyances—and her brutal, violent death. I sat there wondering, thinking—no, maybe even becoming envious. The overriding thought that came to my mind was, 'How lucky.'

"Yes, how lucky were the Pryors to have this community of support, to have been able to have not one or two but multiple services, events, and celebrations of Sarah's life with the love and support of so many and now, finally, to be able to put her bones to rest, to say good-bye to Sarah and to be joined by so many who had been with them since the moment Sarah was gone from their Wayland home just a tad too long that October day 12-plus years ago. How lucky! Why lucky? What I realized is that I grew up in an environment of people who ached—ached to 'find the bones' and to put them to rest in a final resting place.

"I grew up as a child of the Holocaust. Friends, relatives, hundreds, thousands, millions died brutal, violent deaths. Before they were killed, they, like Sarah, were "missing." But, no community searched for them. There was no service, no dedication, no celebration, and no resting place. Parents could not, as we think we can, "protect" their children. The community at large did not care. No one was found. No one was identified. No one was buried. No one was given a 'final resting place.'

"The numbers were so large, the brutality so cruel, the upheaval so enormous that no supporting, loving community remained to offer a kind, helping hand, to cry out against the violence, to find purpose in the suffering and in the dying. No community remained to carve out the positives that could be gained from the destruction, pain, and evil of the Holocaust. Mothers, fathers, children, sisters, brothers, grandparents, cousins, aunts, uncles, nieces, nephews—

all were abused, maimed, and killed. Survivors stayed alive through pure will, faith, and through endless hardship. Each individual had so many profound losses that there was little left to offer each other. Survivors were uprooted. And, when it was "all over" they were in new lands with new languages, new jobs, new customs. They were in communities that could not believe the atrocities, who could not fathom the pain, the losses, or the suffering. The only alternative was to try to forget—to pretend it never happened—to forge a new life.

"My parents forged this new life. They talked little of their Nazi experiences. They attended no memorials, no "celebrations," no funerals for Nazi victims. They found no resting places for their murdered family and friends. And I, I am a product of the "new life." Born in America in 1945, I am the first-born American in my family. My sister, nine years my senior, was born in Germany in 1936. Their immigration and the war came between us. Need I say more? We were born on different continents to markedly different families. I was born free, yet the losses of the past haunted my life as if I had been there.

"Today at Sarah's funeral there was a plea to remember what Sarah has 'taught' us—to love, to forgive, to live each day to its fullest, to enjoy. But, Sarah re-emphasized to me that one must remember, mourn, and say good-bye with as many loved ones, as large a community around us, as possible. It's just plain 'okay' to have many weep together.

"I had my opportunity to weep this past summer when, on July 29, 1997, I returned to Fürth, Germany, my parents' hometown, to attend a memorial service for the 887 Jews from Fürth who were murdered during World War II. About 60 people came, 35 elderly Fürthers who returned to Fürth (some for the first time in 60 years), and 25 Fürth offspring. The sixty of us came from all over the world, from the United States, Canada, Argentina, South Africa, England, Ireland, Israel, Switzerland, Sweden, France and more. We gathered at the new Jewish cemetery to say, 'good-bye.' Seeing Aryan, German newscasters and photographers putting on yarmulkes so that their heads would be covered in a holy place, hearing beautiful Hebrew songs being sung loudly in a land that arrested you and killed you just for being Jewish were in themselves moving and powerful. Being able to say good-bye to my uncle, my father's brother, whom I never met and who was murdered by the Nazis in 1942 made it real. Name after name, picture after picture, story after story. We were able to say, 'Good-bye.' It was healing.

"Today I found a new meaning to healing. We have not just said, 'Good-bye,' to Sarah Pryor, we have put her to rest. It is somehow easier to put one person to rest than to grasp, understand, and put 6-12 million to rest. Numbers, not names, haunt us. The power of the Fürth Memorial, as the Sarah Pryor funeral, is that numbers became names, a community came together in a shared grief to mourn its losses, it was "okay" to cry, and we found a resting place for our loved ones in a memorial wall in the town where they had lived. My uncle and his fellow Fürthers had, in their own way, come home to rest.

"And, so, I went to Sarah Pryor's funeral today so that I could offer support to a family I have grown to love. And, instead, I got a new understanding, a profound insight into the yearning I have had to find a final resting place for members of my family who were murdered in Germany during the Holocaust.

"I am glad that Sarah has come home to her final resting place."

—Evy Davis

[21] NOTES OF COMFORT

Charlie Austin & The News

AFTER SARAH'S FUNERAL, Charlie Austin, our dear compassionate TV reporter friend, added his lovely baritone to the burial service with his heart-felt and moving rendition of "Amazing Grace."

Local television news stations—including WBZ TV, Channel 4; WCVB TV, Channel 5; and WHDH TV Channel 7; all preempted network programming to air the funeral from 11:00 a.m. to 12:30 p.m. New England Cable also carried it live. The decision to cover the service at Trinitarian Congregational Church seemed natural, news directors said.

"Far more people wished to attend than could crowd into the church and church annex and the news media had an unusually gracious invitation from the Pryor family to televise the event," they said. WCVB News Director Candy Altman said, "In fact, Mrs. Pryor was very clear it was a way for the community to share in this (as they) have been such a help to the family the past years. It was also an easy decision for reporters and editors who had been with the case since the beginning and invested something of themselves in it. There is a different level of connection here. It's hard to explain what you feel in your heart. It just felt like the right thing to do."

WBZ TV News Director Peter Brown said that the Pryor story forever changed child rearing, and that was part of his decision to air the service.

New England Cable News Station Manager Charlie Kravetz said that Sarah Pryor, like other well-known public figures, worked her way into every household in the state. "People have made the (Pryors) part of their lives. This was an opportunity to create that rare kind of collective community through television. It is one of the things television is good at."

SARAH'S FUNERAL WAS reported on by newspapers as well. On January 14, 1998, Michael Kunzelman reported in the *Middlesex News* as follows:

Police feel obligated to solve Pryor Case

"Over the years, the police and prosecutors on the Pryor case grew into a tight-knit family. The Pryors in turn, welcomed investigators into their extended family. Barbara handed framed pictures of her daughter to all the investigators on Sarah's case. The picture adorned their desks for years.

"'More times than he would care to remember,' Wayland's former police chief Thomas O' Loughlin had the unenviable job of notifying Sarah's parents whenever a promising tip lead to another dead end in the search for their missing daughter. 'Every time you'd hang up the phone you'd feel like crying. But, they always surprised me. They would console me—I know I am a better person for knowing the Pryors. They taught me to cherish every moment with my children. Sarah is like our child. I'll never forget her.'"

Sarah's funeral was aired throughout New England. In the weeks after, our family received more than three hundred sympathy cards and letters, mostly from caring people we have yet to meet. Television station WCVB, Channel 5, reported receiving more than 200 calls in appreciation for being able to view the farewell service for our Sarah.

Pastor Saylor

IN THE DAYS that followed, among those sympathy notes we received, I found a heart-warming letter from my minister, Dr. Saylor who had officiated at Sarah's funeral:

Dear Barbara,

I have been thinking, Barbara and all the family are alchemists. The alchemist in the middle ages searched for a way to turn lead into gold. Lead is heavy, dull, a "base metal." They never succeeded, but you have. From something unspeakably evil, and the resulting grief, you have produced gold. The gold of love for life, the gold of service to others, the gold of living faith, the gold of hope. This gold enriches all who know you.

May it give joy to each of you as well.

"Evil is not the final word. Grace is."

Faithfully yours,

Dr. Carl Saylor, Pastor

Trinitarian Congregational Church

Epilogue:

Sharing Sarah's

Song of Love

"Think of the possibility of generosity in the face of loss."

—Anonymous

OPPORTUNITIES TO SERVE in leadership positions in Women's Clubs and Bible Studies have engaged my interest partly because public speaking has always seemed easy for me. Also, as time passed, I wanted to share my experiences in losing Sarah. It seemed important to tell members of law enforcement, criminal justice groups, and members of the media some actions that helped me as a victim of a violent crime.

Although I may have forgotten the names of persons who asked me to speak, I do remember the messages I shared.

I gave various talks in response to invitations from various groups, including an annual Massachusetts Press Association meeting, testimony at a Judicial Committee Hearing at the State House, and at the Exceptional Women Awards Luncheon. In the years of waiting to know what happened to Sarah and after that, I took advantage of my public speaking experience and tried to share what I had learned.

In front of print and visual media professionals I explained that in over more than 12 years of dealings with them and with few exceptions my family and I were treated with respect, courtesy, and cooperation. They are sometimes unfairly criticized as they often have to investigate stories about people who are victims of heart-wrenching crimes. Victims are trying to survive and are not always able to articulate or make well-thought out statements or actions. We talk too much or aren't able to speak our thoughts. It is like we are living a nightmare we can't awaken from and we cannot erase what has happened. I implored them to remember to be patient with victims.

Within days of Sarah's abduction we realized we needed the media in order to get her picture and her story as widely distributed as possible in hopes of locating her and bringing her home. Nothing was more important to us and to the law enforcement community. We wanted to cooperate with the media but we needed the media to respect our vulnerability and our need for privacy in the trauma we were living. I think needless hurt and re-victimization is done to crime victims and their families by careless reporting. I asked them to please remember victims' lives will never be the same. Report your stories with accuracy, truth, and compassion.

In a 1999 Judicial Committee Hearing at the Boston State House I again got to speak on the subject I am so passionate about—victim's rights. In the long journey of being a victim of a violent crime, there have been many bright spots. Most of these have come from the investigative team, the victim's advocates, and many New Englanders who cared about a little girl they never knew. It is important to provide guidance through the criminal justice system process, especially to the young, the elderly, and the disabled. A bill had been proposed that addressed the need to explain, guide, and make the process less frightening. It requested, among other important safeguards for victims of a violent crime, that separate and secure waiting areas be set aside for victims as a place where victims of serious crimes can wait while they navigate the rough waters of the criminal justice system.

Victims and their families are often traumatized by the crime committed against them, and need to summon courage to face their assailants, to testify in court, and need a safe place to retreat to during the long, difficult journey toward justice. Sarah's Place (dedicated in April 1997) is a respite from the stress of the court hearings and painful stories that must be told. The rooms are accessible only to victims and their families, and criminal justice professionals, and offer a quiet, comfortable, and safe space for victims to consult with police officers, prosecutors, and victim advocates. In high-profile cases, the rooms are a haven and protection from the media.

That bill passed in 1999, and there are special rooms set aside for victims and vulnerable witnesses in court houses throughout Massachusetts.

A third opportunity came to share my experience with a wider public. I was surprised and honored along with six other women at the Boston Exceptional Women Awards Luncheon on May 11, 2000. It was to be "a celebration of women who have impressed us with their talents, their compassion, and their perseverance even in the toughest of times." In my acceptance speech, I explained how my family and I were so grateful that so many other people were lifting me and my family up, how countless people throughout New England had been my water wings through sometimes turbulent waters. I accepted the award in memory of Sarah and in honor of all victims of violence, especially children. And in closing shared the words of Beth Neelson, "Say goodnight, not goodbye. You will never leave my heart behind. Like the path of a star, I'll be anywhere you are."

Calls to speak in prison came, which I at times rejected. In one case, my friend Terri said that the men had asked for me to come and give them hopeful words of encouragement. Although they were incarcerated they were privy to the continual news about Sarah Pryor and cared about her. I politely offered excuses as to why I could not visit, meeting her persistence with my steadfast resistance. I was already involved with the women at MCI (Massachusetts Correctional Institution) Framingham. What I did not tell Terri was that a men's prison was not where I ever imagined being. As the victim of a violent crime, the Office for Victims had notified me that Sarah's alleged murderer had been returned to a Texas jail to serve his violation of parole having left Texas and returned to Massachusetts without notifying his parole officer. I didn't want to think about men in any prison. After a long time, reluctantly, I saw that my friend would not give up calling me, asking me, refusing to pay attention to my lame excuses. I agreed to come once to Norfolk prison just to be done with it!

On a Sunday evening in June, 2000, I joined Charlie, the prison chaplain, and another woman as we were escorted to the room where men were playing guitars and singing songs of praise. As I entered I thought how enthusiastic the men seemed in spite of their confinement.

They welcomed me like a long-lost relative, so different from what I had imagined. Soon I began my inspirational talk and watched the men nodding and smiling as they listened to me despite a slight disturbance as an inmate was escorted from the room.

When I finished my talk the men stood and cheered giving me a feeling of such joy. I was greeted and thanked by each participant. Then one of the correctional officers in the room said, "Mrs. Pryor, I am going to ask you and your friends to follow me." My heart sank. I thought, *What have I done wrong? It feels like a summons to the principal's office.* I walked with steps of dread as he led us into a room where an inmate sat at a small table. My heart sank again. The CO invited me to sit in the chair opposite the young man, saying, "The inmate asked for permission to speak to you."

Puzzled by what was happening, I sat in the chair as the young man sitting across from me introduced himself as Michael and asked, "Do you know me?"

"No," I said.

"I am a lifer here in prison. I did not know you were coming today and had to leave the room. I asked to speak to you in private. Because of my record, I was a suspect in your daughter's case and was questioned by the authorities. But, I want to tell you I had nothing to do with that."

Tears began falling down his rugged face. I turned to the CO and said, "Permission to touch Michael's arm?"

When it was granted I tenderly held his outstretched arm, looked into his weeping eyes and said, "I know you didn't. I am glad I came today so we could meet and you could talk with me."

His smile warmed me and lit up the entire room. He asked if he could write to me after our wonderful meeting. I happily agreed.

That prison experience was a life-lesson for me and a lasting memory. When I arrived home after the unanticipated blessing I felt remorse that my initial stubborn refusal to accept the invitation delayed the release of a heavy burden from my new found friend. I was grateful for Terri and her persistence with my hardened heart.

January 1998

THE WAYLAND HIGH School Awards Assembly, first known to us in June of 1988, honored seniors in the class. Byron received the Tommy Raskin Memorial Scholarship. The named scholarships are unique in that "the yearly awards are given to academically successful students who most reflect the character and attributes of the named honoree . . . The Tommy Raskin Memorial Scholarship was established in 1977 as a tribute to Tommy Raskin who died at the age of sixteen. Tommy battled a major illness for four years displaying great courage and optimism throughout. He inspired everyone with whom he came in contact. He exhibited an unusual spirit and love of life. Tommy cherished the everyday things in life that we all take for granted—family, friends, community, and school."

I was proud of Byron and agreed that this scholarship fit his character as he had maintained a hopeful and encouraging spirit through the hard days of Sarah being absent from our daily lives. A seed was planted in my mind. If Sarah was not found I would donate a named scholarship in her honor.

In the late 1990s I gathered friends together and planned a fund-raising event for seed money for the scholarship. We held a "Forget Me Not" dinner and silent auction and invited a hundred people to attend an event at Wayland's Sandy Burr Country Club to raise funds for a memorial scholarship. I crafted the words describing Sarah's character and why she was being memorialized. The Wayland High School Scholarship Committee has awarded twenty scholarships in her honor since 1998. I wrote:

The Sarah Elizabeth Pryor Memorial Scholarship

"This yearly award is given to academically successful students who most reflect the character and attributes of the named honoree. This scholarship is given in loving remembrance of Sarah Pryor. Nine-year-old Sarah had moved with her family to Wayland from Pennsylvania in 1985. Her sister and brother started Wayland High School in September. On October 9th of that year, Sarah was abducted while taking a walk on a beautiful afternoon. Twelve years later a bone fragment was identified as Sarah's and a funeral was held for her on January 13, 1998, on what would have been her 22nd birthday.

"This scholarship honors a student who, like Sarah, was enthusiastic about life, compassionate with people and always eager to help. She worked best in the background, never pushing out into the foreground taking the glory, but encouraged, supported and helped from the sidelines. She loved her family and was filled with faith and hope and charity."

November 2000

TWO YEARS AFTER we buried Sarah's remains, my mother died in Concord, in May, 2000. I had made weekly visits with Mom at her assisted living facility for thirteen years, so that after her death I felt day-after-day of emptiness. Meg was living in Manhattan working as an actress, and Byron and Jennifer lived in Pittsburgh, PA, where they had blessed me with the gift of a grandson, Joshua, in September, 1998. I tried to travel from Boston to Pittsburgh every other month, but I wanted to be nearer my family and to enjoy the delights of being a first-time grandmother. A job possibility appeared late in the year at a position with Mellon Bank in downtown Pittsburgh, so I headed home to Pennsylvania to start a new chapter in my life.

We had come to Boston as a family of five in 1985. Now Meg, Byron, and I made the journey to Pennsylvania driving my car and toting my possessions. Sarah, of course, was noticeably absent and Andy and I were divorced. I thought as we traveled in the southwesterly direction that I was a fortunate woman, grateful for the constant love and support of family and friends, and the concern and care of countless folks whom I would never meet or know. My faith and hope were strong. The years in Massachusetts had given me many blessings and I looked forward to my life back where I had grown up.

Left to right, Jennifer holding Michael as a baby (now 9), Meg, Joshua who is now 21), Drew (now 18), Byron holding Ryan (now 11), and me.

August 2013, Back to Boston

THE PRYOR FAMILY drove back to the Boston area to attend my nephew Brendan's wedding on Cape Cod. After celebrating the wedding and visiting with relatives over the weekend, I went to Cushing, Maine to visit my friend Marilyn while Byron, Jen, their boys, and Meg drove to Wayland to see the "Dog and Sled" sculpture. The joyful, playful spirit of our little girl exemplified in the sculpture beckons children to sit on the Border Collie's back and tail, and to lovingly pat her worn, shiny head. My four grandsons, ages 2-14, were photographed as they explored this wonderful new experience.

Brendon makes a Christmas visit to the "Dog and Sled" sculpture inspired by Sarah.

A more somber trip awaited the family a block from the delight of children enjoying a well-designed playground. In the nearby cemetery is the headstone and grave of Sarah Elizabeth Pryor. Years have passed since we buried Sarah's remains there. My family visited the black, marble stone with Sarah's sweet image engraved into it. There they found pebbles resting atop the headstone and a large plastic bag leaning against it, full of laminated articles from newspapers published at the time of her funeral. A cover sheet of white paper bore this simple message in felt pen:

To Sarah's Family: Her life and her death were important and had a huge impact on all of us. Thank You

When the family returned to Pennsylvania they showed me the note. How glad I was to know that Sarah is still remembered by countless people, strangers to us all.

August 2014, Andy Passes

MY WRITING JOURNAL lay idle for two years while I was engaged in helping Byron and Jennifer with their busy world of four adopted sons, as well as serving as a deacon and on various committees at my church, and spending time with friends.

Byron, Jen and their four boys were vacationing with her parents at Kentucky Lake when the alarming call came. They phoned me in Pittsburgh to say Andy had been in a one-car crash in Ohio and was being air flighted to the Ohio State facility in Columbus where he had been successfully treated for oral cancer the year before.

Andy had remarried and divorced again in the Boston area. He decided in the early 2000s to return to his hometown of Newark, Ohio, where he had spent his childhood, graduating from Newark High and Denison College in Granville. Once back in his hometown he reconnected with old friends, visited Byron and his family several times a year, and was enjoying retirement.

The news this summer day left me speechless and waiting to hear the extent of his injuries. Jen and Byron were hurrying to Columbus. Meg was traveling from New York and asked me to meet her at the Pittsburgh Airport to drive her to the hospital. The medical updates and diagnosis were chilling, cutting so deeply that I could scarcely take them in. According to the specialists, the injuries to his neck and spine were grave, Andy was paralyzed from the shoulders down, he was conscious, in a neck brace following emergency surgery, on life support with breathing and feeding tubes.

Meg and I were quiet, sitting in the car without conversation on the two-hour drive, trying to imagine what would lie before us as we rushed to be with Byron and Jen in Andy's room in the Intensive Care Unit. Once there, the space seemed eerie with beeps of the life support machines and electronic charts visibly recording Andy's vital signs. We hugged Byron and Jen, tears flowing, all of us feeling hopelessness for Andy.

The nurse on staff greeted us warmly and then retired to attend to her duties. Meg went to her dad and he smiled as she talked softly to him.

"Thank you, Lord," I whispered, "that Andy is conscious, he can nod his head, he can smile, he understands what his family and the doctors are saying."

While Meg talked with Andy, Byron and Jen told me more discouraging details. The doctors determined Andy would never breath on his own nor speak or move. He needed a cardiac pacemaker but would not tolerate the implant procedure. His doctors made the prognosis clear to Andy, repeatedly confirming what his End of Life wishes were—Andrew Bell Pryor made it very clear he wished care and comfort only. The nurse went through the paperwork procedures and it was time for us all to say goodbye.

I sat on the far side of the darkened room in shadow as Meg, Byron, and Jen said their farewells. Then I walked to Andy to say what I needed to say. Following my children's lead, I touched Andy's shoulder where he could feel sensation. When I leaned close to his face he smiled, and I knew he recognized me.

"Hi," I said as he maintained his beautiful smile. "I want to tell you three things, Andy. First, I know your children loved you and I know for certain how much you loved Byron, Meg, and Sarah. Next, I am sorry for any way I hurt you, and I hope you will forgive me." Tears rolled down my cheeks as this man I had married and who was the father of my children nodded his head in agreement. Sniffling, wishing I had a tissue, I continued, "And the last thing is this: You get to see Sarah first!"

Andy's face lit up with a big smile. I placed myself with a box of tissues near Meg and Byron who stood with Jen beside their Dad as he peacefully left our lives.

April 2015,
Classmates Remember

WE STILL RECEIVE notes of comfort. Since Sarah went missing, we have always received the care and comfort of so many, and so many stories so beautifully written as they recall the journeys of Sarah's friends, classmates, neighbors, and all who knew her. While they have *all* been dear to me, some touched me so deeply, I wanted to share their beauty with my readers:

Dear Pryor Family,

I am thinking of you, and my prayers are with you during these times. As a fifth grader, I remember Sarah's enjoyment of being in the 4th & 5th grade chorus. Though she was not there long, we were touched by her presence. She loved to sing, and when I think of her I start to sing, "A Few of My Favorite Things" from The Sound of Music. We sang this song in her honor and I think Sarah can still be with us though not in body in spirit. Sarah and you will always remain a part of my life and our community's life.

Thinking of you,

—K. Lynch

The circle of people who actually knew Sarah personally is quite small. They include her immediate family and her extended family, our church families, neighbors, Sarah's classmates at Pleasant Valley Elementary School in Mc Murray, Pennsylvania, and her fourth-grade class at Claypit Hill Elementary School in Wayland. When Sarah moved north she sadly left behind best friends Sarah Johnson (Ohm), Sara Smart (Klein), Lesley Spencer (Hoye), and Miriam Rebold Hahn.

When Lesley and Sara were married they each mailed me copies of the church programs from their weddings. I was happy to hear of their marriages and to learn their new last names—Sara Klein and Lesley Hoye. These women remembered their lost friend by placing a single yellow rose on the altar in her memory, with a note in the wedding program, "The yellow rose on the altar is in memory of Sarah Elizabeth Pryor."

Sarah Smart Klein included this note. "I still think about Sarah. I know that a lot of people loved Sarah. I hope you and your family are doing well. Sarah was remembered in my wedding program, and a flower was placed on the altar in her memory. Love, Sara."

In fact, I was surprised and delighted to receive Facebook *friend requests* from three of Sarah's friends on Facebook:

- Sara Smart Klein (4/12/2015): "I think about Sarah often, and remember what a special friend she was. I have an eight-year-old daughter now, and she is very tall, just like Sarah!"

- Lesley Spencer Hoye: "I have to jump on the bandwagon. Please know, even though it has been so long, you and your family are never far from my thoughts and prayers. I still miss my friend, Sarah. My son is 10, my daughter is 7."

- Sarah Johnson Ohm (4/13/2015): "There is not a day that goes by, that I don't think about Sarah, and the beautiful girl she was. What an amazing friend she was. My yard is full of daffodils, and I await their bloom, here in Minnesota, in a week or two. These beautiful yellow flowers always remind me of Sarah. Her song is such an important part of mine."

And Sarah Johnson Ohm wrote the following piece in memory of Sarah:

At Miss Rusinko's backyard wedding reception. From left to right, friend, Sarah Pryor (tallest), Sarah Johnson (Ohm), Miriam Rebold Hahn.

Glimpse of Sarah Pryor

Daffodils, Blond Hair, Beautiful Smile, Gentle, Caring Soul

"AS SPECIAL AS that was to be invited to our 2nd-grade teacher's wedding (Miss Rusinko), I remember the lovely reception in the side yard of the church, mingling with the adults and feeling fancy with our classmates. Sarah wore a beautiful long dress that was as lovely as she was.

"I was crushed when I heard that Sarah was moving. My whole life was in Peters Township and I couldn't imagine anyone ever leaving. It was a surreal feeling, starting the new school year without Sarah there. It was almost as if she was just on vacation. In a strange twist of fate, my new "best" friend, Stacey Wilcock (a new girl who had just moved from New Hampshire) had met Sarah that summer at a summer camp. It was almost as though Stacey was in my life to be my Sarah connection. Stacey and I have remained best friends—and maybe that's another way that Sarah's presence is always with me.

"I don't recall how I learned of Sarah's abduction, nor do I know when I was told. I imagine I was shielded from it by my parents as best as they could. As a 4th-grade kid, I guess I just always assumed that Sarah would come back. After all, she was just on vacation, right? Denial or avoidance or naivety, I don't know what it was, but I felt from that point on that I was in a cloud when I talked about Sarah, that it wasn't really real.

"I remember a presentation that the girls and I did at PV (Pleasant Valley Elementary School in Mc Murray, Pennsylvania) when we were in 5th grade. The beautiful painting of a blond little girl at the merry go round holding balloons. I wonder how in the world I was able to speak in front of the whole school. I had such an immense fear of speaking in public, there were a number of events throughout my childhood that I backed out of for fear of being on stage. Anyway, I remember being at the school the day before to practice with the other girls and our moms. And that's it. I don't remember the speech I don't remember the actual moment. I'm certain it was Sarah that was with me to give me the courage to talk with our school.

"The years went on, the daffodils bloomed, and I always thought of Sarah. Praying and hoping that she would return home safely. After all, she was just on vacation…

"I was a senior in college when I found out what really happened to Sarah. I remember getting a letter and opening it up excited for mail. It was from my mom. When I saw the finality of the newspaper it was real. When I read the contents I dropped to my knees and started bawling, right in the middle of the commons. It was real. She wasn't on vacation. It was the first time in my entire life I remember feeling the true grief of her loss. I didn't realize until that moment how much I had kept inside. There have been numerous moments since that I am numb with sadness and loss. Yet also an equal number of times when I think about the amazing person she was and how lucky I am to have known her.

"True friendship, love, adventure, strong relationships, living every day to the fullest. I cherish the moments with my own children and hold them as close as I can.

My daughter is in 3rd grade, 9 years old—I couldn't even imagine if…

"I have a picture of Sarah that I look at often. It is one from perhaps a family picture of you all from church. She is so sweet, so full of life and beauty. She is with us; she is certainly with us."

—Sarah Johnson Ohm

Thoughts from Sarah Johnson Ohm's Mom

"Dearest Sissy. My memories of the turbulent time with the loss of Sarah Pryor thirty years ago are…

"Prior to the news of Sarah's abduction, you were an easy-going, no care-in-the-world type of child. This changed dramatically after you were gently filled in on what had happened to your best friend, Sarah, who had recently moved to Boston. I remember that you became so stoic and would not talk about it for years. You never cried. You avoided the topic altogether as if you didn't even care. I knew that the hurt was so deep that you were just too young and unable to process it. The telling sign of your grief and love was the silent reminder of Sarah Pryor's framed picture that remains on your dresser… even to this day. I prayed that someday you would be able to come to grips with the ugly reality of Sarah's abduction and death, that you would not blame God but would be reconciled, knowing the sins of this world, and that you and Sarah were children of God, and not of this world, and also that you would someday be at peace, knowing that God lifted Sarah up from her time of terror into His loving arms, where she will remain with Him, and will someday be reunited with her family and loved ones.

"Following the news of Sarah's abduction, you became fearful of everything and everyone. You crouched and crawled under the un-draped windows of our family room and kitchen, to make sure that no one (out in the woods) would see you. You refused to be by yourself in the house. You told me that you did not want to have children when you grew up, and you turned down every opportunity to babysit... up until you were a about a senior in high school.

"I prayed that God would release you from your fears, knowing that you were chosen by Him to someday be the most wonderful mother and teacher ever! Oh yes, the presentation at PV boggled my mind. You were given a strength and presence of mind as if carried on angel's wings.

"Now you, Sarah Smart, and Leslie Spencer have "found" Barbara Pryor at the same time. This is not a coincidence by any stretch of imagination. This was meant to happen, to give new life and meaning for you three "children," and for Barbara and her family. It is truly a gift from God.

"I love you more than you can ever know! The daffodils are blooming here, as well.

"Love, Mom"

Remembering Sarah by Miriam Rebold Hahn

MIRIAM, Sarah's friend, now lives in Dachau, Germany with her husband and children. We communicate by e-mail. Miriam wrote this essay about her friend, Sarah and sent it to me.

"Today, 30 years after Sarah's death, I am a mother of three in Germany with my husband, Raphael. I'm a freelance graphic designer who sometimes attempts to pursue my hobbies of refinishing old furniture, making music and getting back into hip-hop dancing. However, lack of space and the daily grind are always surefire distractions to accomplishing any of those, so I spend most of my time taking care of the household and the three blessings the Lord has given us and working from home.

"In the back of my mind, though, is an ongoing plan to get something else done, anything else! I love the Lord, and I trust that He took me out of the warm southern state of North Carolina (where I had lived since I was 13) for a reason (it better be a good one!). And I thank God for WhatsApp[1], which keeps me in touch with my family pretty much every day.

"Although we were very young when Sarah was taken from us, I still remember her smile and that she was absolutely one of the sweetest friends I had. There was a time when we even called each other best friends. (Of course, when you are in elementary school, that happens a lot.) I remember the water dam near her house, where she loved to go with a picnic and enjoy the nature. She was brave and adventurous, and smart! There is a photo of three of us friends at our 2nd grade teacher's wedding. One thing really stands out—Sarah. She towers above the other two of us, and she's dressed in white, her face reminds me of a beautiful roman statue and she looks like a goddess. I didn't see her that way at the time, she was always just Sarah, and I surely took her for granted as most children do each other.

"I very clearly remember hearing of Sarah's abduction I even remember what I was doing—riding the morning school bus. It was not long after she had moved away, and Monica Caldwell, a mutual friend said, "Did you hear that Sarah Pryor has been

---

[1] WhatsApp Messenger is a freeware, cross-platform messaging and Voice over IP service owned by Facebook. It allows users to send text messages and voice messages, make voice and video calls, and share images, documents, user locations, and other media. — Wikipedia

kidnapped?" It still gives me the chills today. I didn't believe it though. When a child hears something horrible about a child that moved away, it seems made up, because that child is far away. I was skeptical.

"'How do you know?' I said.

"I couldn't fathom how anybody here would already know what happened there. I didn't think at the time that phone calls travel at the speed of light when tragedy hits. When it was confirmed by enough other people, I thought about her family, a lot. I imagined what they're feeling, what her older brother and sister are doing without her, and what Sarah could be going through. I asked the Lord to save her. I imagined what it would be like if it had been me. I too have an older brother and sister. After that, I eventually put it out of my head, because there was nothing I could do with this horrible information. I hoped that she would be found safe, and then I blocked it out. Occasionally, a rumor would go around that Sarah had been spotted somewhere, like a runaway. I hoped it was true, and that she would be brought home.

"Thirteen years later we had moved to North Carolina, and one day my father handed me an article about the discovery of Sarah's remains. The confirmation that she was not a runaway and that something unspeakable was the end of my beautiful, sweet angel of a friend hit me like a ton of bricks. To this day, that bitter truth will not sink in. It's a solemn reminder, that this fallen world we live in is evil. Sure, the Lord is among us, He is our Deliverer and our Helper, our Comforter… but we face evil until He finally puts an end to it and takes His children home, to where Sarah is.

"Thinking back, not that I would have wished it upon anybody, and pardon my French, but there were so many spoiled, insensitive little "bitties" in school, why did the Lord choose to take one of best people among us? Doesn't make any sense to me.

"The lessons I have learned from the whole journey are simple and redundant: Love your loved ones and treat them well while you still have the chance! And the Lord is in control even when it seems like everything is out of control."

—Miriam Rebold Hahn

IT WAS FROM Sarah's father's simple words that I drew the biggest lesson. Andrew recalled how as he would leave the house he would look back at the family room window and see Sarah inside, dancing. He loved gardening and had a big garden in Pennsylvania where the family lived before moving to Wayland.

"Sarah, he said, "would come down in the morning and tell me the neighborhood pool was open—'It's time to go swimming!' I just thank God I had enough sense to put down the hoe and go."

That is the message of Sarah's life—to take the time to love. To set down the hoes, look up from television or the computer, and appreciate the people who are most important in our lives. And we can hope in time the image of Sarah's face will be a reminder of what we should savor in this world and not what we have lost.

Co-worker Joanne Elison-Wood had the idea to create Sarah as an angel from a sketch Joanne made from a photo on my desk (taken by Miss McNamara), which became Sarah's headstone.

CLOSING THOUGHTS

I HAVE LEARNED valuable lessons for understanding the burdens that people carry while suffering loss. Some of these lessons came from books I read while struggling to understand how to go on living. Here are some guidelines that have helped me to listen better and encourage those who are trying to "keep on keeping on" in the face of their physical or emotional losses.

1. Decide to "go on."
2. Let go of anger, hate, and resentment. They crowd out your love, joy, and peace.
3. Look outward with hope rather than turning feelings inward.
4. Don't try to make sense of what is senseless.
5. Honor the beauty of your lost one's spirit; do not let evil destroy it.

6. Think of what you *can* do to honor your lost one despite realizing you are powerless to alter what has happened to you, your child, and your family.

7. Do not play the *what if* game. It is useless and robs you of energy and hope.

8. Remember, the more a person was loved, the longer the grieving takes.

9. Don't rush your grief or allow others to rush you.

10. Respect everyone's unique way of grieving.

11. Let people help you bear your burden. It is a gift they want to give.

12. Let people take care of you in your moments of need.

13. Let people know when you are having a fragile day. They are not mind readers.

14. Think of ways that trusted ones can help you keep the light of hope burning when you have moments of doubt and fear.

15. Forgive yourself and others. Forgiveness is called a gift because it frees you of destructive thoughts and potentially destructive actions.

16. Forgive others for insensitive remarks, unwanted advice, or even silence. Remember they may be uncomfortable not knowing what to say.

17. Be quick to listen, slow to speak, and slow to anger. (James 1: 1-5)

18. Be in a continual spirit of both gratitude and cooperation for those professionals working in your behalf, criminal justice and mental health workers, media.

19. Remember that there is no scale that measures anyone's pain!

20. People may mean well, but they can say hurtful things.

21. I have decided that it is easier for me to believe people mean well, have good intentions, and want to be helpful than to believe they say careless and

hurtful things on purpose. If you are giving your opinion your words can sound as though you have all the answers when certainly you do not.

A partial list of some remarks that have not been helpful:

- "Sarah disappeared." She did not disappear or vanish! Those words were offensive to me and were used repeatedly by the media. What happened was not magic ... she was taken!
- "Sarah was in the wrong place at the wrong time." No, she was walking near home on a beautiful day as she should have been able to do. Evil was present through no fault of this child!
- "I know how you feel because . . ." Your loss is *yours*; you don't know mine!
- "God never gives a burden more than one can bear." You know God's motives?
- "At least you have two other children." Yes, having other children gives you some comfort, but the pain of the missing one remains. Don't try to make other innocent sufferers fill the empty space.
- Be careful about beginning your sentences with, "At least," or "Well." That usually means you are giving advice or you are judging from your own experience.
- "God must have needed her." Well, I need her with me! Another terrible statement which claims you know God's motives!
- "I couldn't handle what you are enduring."
- "I've taught my children not to talk to strangers."
- "At least you have closure." Closure is a loaded word. No bereaved parent ever has closure. Our lives are forever unalterably changed. Things can get better but we live with damaged lives. Meg,

Byron, Andy and I give testimony to a new normal, but we do not have or want "closure."

Adjusting to a New Way of Living

Doug Manning's book, *Don't Take My Grief From Me*, helped me understand better how I grieved the loss of Sarah. The statement, "The more you loved a person and were loved by them the longer the grieving," altered my thinking and gave me permission to know that grief was going to last a long time.

My friend Diane also helped me when she wrote me a note after Sarah was first missing: "You have a gaping wound now. I promise you that it will close someday, but you will always have a scar. Some days you will not remember the hurt, but sometimes the pain will remind you of your deep "forever" wound." This friend's wisdom was very helpful.

As a victim of a violent crime, I suffer from post-traumatic stress disorder (PSTD). My symptoms when full-blown are sleeplessness, a startle reflex, feelings of anxiety, and intense pain in my jaw (TMJP). Newspaper and television news items trigger these responses when I hear or read reports of violence, especially against children. Byron and Meg have censored movies and books that they think I should avoid. In extreme cases, my body shakes and I experience spastic and uncontrollable sobbing. At those times the way to peace for me is to let the feelings out— let them rip as I feel emotional pain. I have learned to ask someone to be with me to remind me to breathe.

When the stormy minutes pass, I can return to a version of normal.

January 2015,
Melody at the Market

IN AISLE 3, searching for my favorite liquid hand soap, I thought I heard the song while shoppers passed me with carts full of groceries. I smiled knowing I had to be correct. It was Jefferson Airplane's 1980s song, "Sara," playing on the piped-in music overhead.

I stood listening to every word, singing the chorus under my breath, "Sara, Sara, No time is a good time for goodbye." This was a serendipitous gift to me, while I anticipated her 39th birthday on January 13th.

SARAH'S SUSPECTED
MURDERER

THE CRIMINAL INVESTIGATION team assigned to Sarah Pryor's case included some of the finest law enforcement professionals available to solve this long-standing mystery. Based on circumstantial evidence they think that John Whirty stalked Sarah (may even have watched her walking the day before) and seized his opportunity to snatch her from heavily trafficked (Route 126) Concord Road. He is a convicted pedophile and was sentenced for the murder of a 14-year old Texas girl in 1967. After serving 17 years of his life sentence in a Texas jail he was paroled in 1984 on good behavior. Whirty left Texas without parole board permission and returned to his home town, less than 15 miles from Wayland. He became a suspect in Sarah's case when he was apprehended after a failed attempt to kidnap a young woman in November 1985, a month after Sarah's abduction.

He served time in Norfolk MCI, for the attempted kidnapping then was returned to prison in Huntsville, Texas, for violating the conditions of his parole. In the years since Whirty has had at least ten parole hearings. Our family and friends have exercised our rights as Victims of Violence and written letters protesting his release, telling the members of the Texas Parole Board how this violent crime has affected our family, friends, and communities. We believe he continues to be a threat to more girls, families, and communities should he be granted parole. We are grateful that the Texas Parole Board has thus far denied him release on parole.

SARAH'S SONG
LIVES ON PROGRAM

SARAH'S SONG SINGS ON- Part II

30th Anniversary PROGRAM

Saturday, October 10, 2015: 7:00 – 10:00

Sandy Burr Golf Club Wayland, MA

Gathering

Introduction Candy O' Terry

Welcome: Barbara Pryor

Moment of Silence in Honor of Sarah's Dad, Andy Pryor

Opening Remarks: Barbara Pryor

Thanksgiving for and Recognition of friends of Sarah and Her Family:

Recognize Byron, Jen, Meg, Carroll & Bob Sandel; Friends from Pleasant Valley Elementary, Mc Murray, PA (Sarah Johnson Ohm, Sara Smart Klein, Lesley Spencer Hoye); Claypit Hill Elementary, Wayland (Christina and Mary Beth Markunas).

The Criminal Justice Team: Wayland PD, Gerry Galvin, Steve Williams, Sandy O'Brien, Ruth Backman;

Middlesex District Attorney's Office: Tom Reilly, Joe Flaherty, John McEvoy, Joe Moynihan, Peter Sennet; Massachusetts State Police; Office of the Attorney General, Commonwealth of MA, Lucy Murray Brown, Janet Fine, Marcia Hill.

Television, Radio and Written Media

WORD FM, Candy O'Terry; The Boston Globe, Bella English; The Middlesex News, Tom Moroney; Charlie Austin, WBZ TV; Susan Wornick and Eileen Prose

The Sarah Pryor Living Memorial Committee and *Nancy Schon: Empty Sled Statue: Kathy Arena, Leslie and Mark Corner, Lee Dawson,

Wayland High School Scholarship Committee Sarah Elizabeth Pryor Memorial Scholarship, *Phyllis Kennedy and Suzanne Tiberi

TJX /T.J. Maxx , Ben Camarrata and all associates, especially Lee Dawson and Julie Parsons.

Friends/Faith Communities Trinitarian Congregational, Pastor Carl Saylor; Church of the Holy Spirit, Revs. Anne and Cassius Webb; Trinity Episcopal Church, Concord; Carroll Sandel, Jan and Carl Turnquist; St Zephrians Church, now Good Shepherd Parish, Ed and Lorna Hebert; Cursillio friends, especially Sylvia Jacobsen and Diane Morrisette.

BARBARA SMITH PRYOR

Solo: Amazing Grace, Candy O' Terry

Closing Remarks: Barbara Pryor

GET IN TOUCH

"I want for readers to be easily able to be in touch with me. I thrive on that—way ahead of speaking engagements, interviews, publicity, etc.! This is my gift, reaching people and listening to their stories as a way of encouraging the discouraged. Please let us not lose sight of this desire of mine."

—Barbara Pryor, Author

Barbara is always happy to hear from readers and looks forward to hearing from you! Send written correspondence to:

Barbara S. Pryor

P.O. Box 4971

Pittsburgh, PA 15206

Email Barbara: missingsarahpryor@gmail.com

ACKNOWLEDGMENTS

I AM BLESSED to have my family who has walked every step of the long Sarah journey with me. You have comforted me and listened to me in my sadness and gladness. Thank you all for being there for me each day. I want to express my forever gratitude to my sister Carroll, you were the "wind beneath my wings," lightening the burden, holding on to me in joy and sorrow.

Nancy Schon, Evy Davis Meygerman, Sarah Ohm, her Mom, and Miriam Hahn, your original compositions that you shared touched me deeply, I wanted to share their beauty with my readers. Thank you.

I am deeply grateful for the countless friends, known to me or not, who have cared about Sarah and my family.

The professionals who comprised Sarah's investigative team were dedicated and competent. Thanks to then District Attorney, Tom Reilly, Wayland Chief of Police Gerry Galvin, Wayland detectives, Sandy O' Brien, and

Steve Williams. You worked steadfastly at trying to find answers while loving our little girl even though you never knew her personally. We are fortunate that the Wayland Police Department, the Massachusetts State Police, the FBI members assigned to the case, and the Boston Middlesex District Attorneys and their staff, worked together without walls or territories in a best practice of cooperation and collaboration. I appreciate all of you, especially, Peter Sennett, Joe Flaherty, John McEvoy, Kevin O'Shea, Dick Baker, Lucy Murray Brown, Marcia Hill and the late Joe Moynihan, Leo Burdick, and Tom O'Loughlin.

To Sarah's classmates who have not forgotten her, from Pleasant Valley School in Mc Murray, Pennsylvania, especially Sarah Johnson Ohm, Lesley Spencer Hoye, Sara Smart Klein, and Miriam Rebold Hahn, and Sarah's class at Claypit Hill School in Wayland, Massachusetts, especially, Christina Markunas, I dearly love each one of you.

My compassionate Bradford Schools, Inc, coworkers and friends I left in Pittsburgh as I journeyed to Boston: Ruth Black, Jackie Boyd Garbet, Lisa Fulton, Lynne Fedorka, Mary Ann Brown, Helen Kaplan and Lucy Mc Laughlin.

I am indebted to the Home Office T J Maxx family who helped make my work days productive with your support and caring, especially for CEO, Ben Cammarata for wanting me to work for you at TJ Maxx, and especially to my archivist and researcher Julie Parsons, Lee Dawson, Kim Coburn, and Geralyn Kolakowski. You remain my forever friends.

Special thanks to Nancy Schon and the "Little Engine That Could"- Sarah Pryor Memorial Committee who helped raise funds for the Nancy Schon sculpture, "Dog and Sled", in the Hannah Williams Park and raised seed money to establish a perpetual Named Scholarship for Sarah at Wayland High School, Wayland, Massachusetts. What an accomplishment to bring delight to many children who play in the playground and hug Sarah's dog! I thank each one of you!

To the communities of faith - you have my praise and thanks, especially Trinitarian Congregational Church, Church of the Holy Spirit, Saint Zephiran's Church, and the Cursillo Community in Massachusetts, the Bethany Nuns, Dr. Carl Saylor, The Reverends Anne and Cassius Webb, The Reverend David Jones, The Reverend Hillary Bercovicci and The Reverend Christopher Leighton. You were special gifts to us in our times of need.

And to my dear church friends from Peter's Township Saint David's Episcopal Church in Pennsylvania, your friendships helped build a foundation for my long journey in Boston.

I give tribute to the professionals in the media who cared about my family first, and the story to be gathered second. I have you in my heart, especially, Bella English, Tom Moroney, Elizabeth Lofty, Kathie Neff Ragsdale, Natalie Jacobson and Chet Curtis, Susan Wornick, Eileen Prose, Candy O' Terry, and the late Charlie Austin and Martie Sender.

As a first-time author, the formidable journey ahead of me was made doable with an incredible team of capable/willing individuals who guided me with their counsel and tireless encouragement.

Debbie Macomber, you are an inspiration to me, I am thankful that I have read every book you have written, this year's new one in a day!

Julie Parsons, co-worker, BFF since 1988 – you first started inputting my writings as a Sarah journal and have stayed by my side cheering me on all these many years. You share in my victory! I love you!

What a joy to meet Anka Kovacevic. I marvel at the beautiful book cover you designed for Missing Sarah. Jerry Cibley, my forever- friend. Your gift creating the posters within two days of Sarah going missing helped the public begin to look for her across the Boston area. Sarah is your Poster Child. Thanks for enrolling Ray Cohen, from RMC Printing in Stoughton for helping us with all the posters.

Rodney Miles, you helped me have my dream realized, delivery of my first book to be published. Because of your incredible efforts and belief in me, Sarah's story may encourage many folks. I am so thankful.

Thank you to our invaluable beta readers: Lynn Cox, Christina Markunas, Lauren Uhl, Patrick Flavin, Gail Reichert, Angela B, Sarah Ohm, Lucy Monteleone, and Nancy Johansen.

Lastly, I am thankful for the gift of my friend who traveled a similar path, my wonderful advisor, co-helper, and editor Elizabeth Philipps. Beyond our shared tragedy we are blessed in knowing each other. You were continually encouraging me, "Keep on...Keeping on!" Thank you I love you beyond measure.

If I have neglected to mention any, please accept my apology. You are in my heart!

I acknowledge God's Grace to be with me every moment of every day.

Sarah's Song Sings On

I am creating something new in you,
a bubbling spring of Joy that spills over into other's lives...
permeating you with Love, Joy and Peace.
—Sarah Young, *Jesus Calling*